Phonics Plus, Se

Contents

Contents Continued

Introduction

Learning to read can be a difficult task. Recent research indicates that many children are struggling as they try to grasp the rudiments of a confusing system of letters, sounds, and words. The United States government grew concerned by the number of children emerging from school who lacked a reading foundation and comprehension skills. In response, Congress issued a mandate that no child should be left behind in the classroom. As a result, teachers, children, parents, and government are working together to make sure that every child becomes a successful reader.

The National Reading Panel (NRP), a group of educators selected to act on behalf of the government, reviewed numerous reports and studies to determine the important elements essential to reading success. In 2001, the panel published *Put Reading First: The Research Building Blocks for Teaching Children to Read.* The report identified five areas critical to reading development: phonemic awareness, phonics, vocabulary, fluency, and comprehension.

The Five Reading Essentials

• **Phonemic Awareness** involves hearing and identifying the individual sounds, or phonemes, in words and understanding that sounds can be manipulated to create new words.

• **Phonics** focuses on the letters of the alphabet and their relationship to spoken sounds.

• **Vocabulary** refers to the words that we hear, speak, read, and write that help us communicate.

• **Fluency** is the ability to read a text silently or orally with accuracy and speed.

• **Comprehension** is being able to understand the words and the purpose of a selection.

While the NRP identified five separate areas of reading instruction, it also determined that all five skills need to be taught in conjunction with one another to further ensure reading success.

The Phonics Plus Series

This reproducible phonics series supplements many recognized phonics programs, yet still implements the other four reading elements identified by the NRP. As a phonics series, the information is presented in a systematic order and provides explicit instruction. Each unit contains phonemic awareness activities for the key phonics skill. Moreover, each phonics skill is supported with a small booklet that children can make and read. Vocabulary, fluency, and comprehension development activities help to further reinforce the phonics skill.

Organization of *Phonics Plus*

This book is divided into seven units. The first unit reviews consonant sounds. The second and third units focus on short and long vowels. The fourth and fifth units provide practice using blends and digraphs. In unit six, children explore *r*-controlled vowels and the sounds of *y* when it is a vowel. Finally, children learn about vowel digraphs and diphthongs in unit seven. The unit components are explained below.

• **Planner** A chart at the beginning of each unit outlines the phonics skills and activities that can be completed during the unit. The chart formatting is easy to read and can be reviewed quickly to note the activities accompanying the unit. It identifies phonemic awareness activities, a skill-specific phonics activity, the vocabulary words for the related story, and the name of the story. Moreover, the planner lists short writing activities that will help reinforce each letter and sound.

• **Teacher Information** A two-page spread following the planner provides explicit instructions for completing the activities listed in the planner. A section is devoted to phonemic awareness activities and phonics activities. The information also guides activities to be used prior to reading, during reading, and after reading the unit story. These ideas support the essential skills of fluency, vocabulary, and comprehension. The teacher information also provides writing ideas to support creative use of words. Finally, these pages suggest activities that will help children apply their knowledge of phonics as they share the unit story at home.

• **Phonics** Activity pages blend the familiar skill pages with fun activities consisting of riddles, crossword puzzles, and word finds. On many pages, children have the opportunity to write a sentence so they are applying phonics skills in a new format.

• **Vocabulary** One page explores some of the words in the unit story. This page explores a vocabulary skill, such as synonyms, antonyms, words with multiple meanings, context, or dictionary skills. The words were chosen to support a specific vocabulary skill. So, you may wish to review the story in advance to select other words children may find challenging.

• **Story** A story was selected to support the phonics skills in each unit. You can duplicate the eight-page story so that each child can have a personal copy. Each phonics skill is included in the story, and the skill words are noted on the teacher information component.

Other Components

• **Assessments** A vowel assessment and consonant blend assessment can be found on pages 5 and 6, respectively. These assessments can be administered at the beginning of the school year to gauge children's phonetic knowledge. After completing the phonics program, children can retake the test to determine their progress.

• **Blackline Masters** The planner suggests fun, hands-on activities that support each phonics skill, such as creating flip books or crossword puzzles. The patterns for these activities can be found on pages 149 through 153. The teacher information component details how to use the blackline masters.

• **Writer's Dictionary Page** A dictionary page can be found on page 154. Several activities suggest that children write words or draw pictures whose names contain a phonics sound in the Writer's Dictionary. It is suggested that you make a 26-page personal "dictionary" for each child using this page. Have children color the letter in the margin to show the alphabet page in their dictionary. Additional pages can be copied and inserted if children need more room to write.

We hope you enjoy this new and exciting phonics product. It is sure to complement any phonics program you choose!

How to Assemble the Stories

1. Reproduce the story pages as they appear in this book. For each story: photocopy pages 2/7 on the back of pages 8/cover; photocopy pages 4/5 on the back of pages 6/3.

2. Place pages 4/5 on top of pages 2/7.

3. Fold the story in half so that pages 4/5 face each other and the cover is on the outside.

4. Staple the book together along the outer left edge.

Assessment: Vowels

Darken the circle beside the word that completes each sentence. Then write the word on the line.

1	Mom takes us to the _____ shop.	○ pat ○ pit ○ pet
2	We want to find a little _____.	○ dig ○ dug ○ dog
3	We _____ the white pup best.	○ like ○ lone ○ lace
4	We take it _____ with us.	○ home ○ hike ○ heat
5	The pup jumps out of the _____.	○ corn ○ car ○ curl
6	It runs to the door of the _____.	○ hound ○ house ○ horse
7	The pup barks with _____.	○ boys ○ toys ○ joy
8	We all laugh at our _____ pet.	○ noise ○ notes ○ new

Assessment: Consonant Blends

Darken the circle beside the word that completes each sentence. Then write the word on the line.

1

_____

Uncle Blake owns a food _____.

○ stick
○ stump
○ store

2

_____

He sells green _____.

○ giraffes
○ grapes
○ grades

3

_____

There is a sale on purple _____.

○ plums
○ plus
○ planes

4

_____

Uncle Blake wears a _____ apron.

○ whale
○ white
○ wheat

5

_____

He cuts the cheese with a _____.

○ knee
○ knock
○ knife

6

_____

He lets me _____ the cheese.

○ wrap
○ wren
○ wrist

7

_____

Sometimes, I get a _____ to eat.

○ snack
○ snake
○ slick

8

_____

Uncle Blake's store is _____.

○ grill
○ grand
○ grade

Unit 1 Planner
Consonants

Lesson	Phonemic Awareness	Phonics	Vocabulary	Comprehension and Fluency	Writing
Lesson 1 Initial Consonants	**Phoneme Manipulation:** Substitute the beginning sound in words	Word Building with Initial Consonants Activity Pages 10–11			Write tongue twisters using words that have the same beginning consonant sound.
Lesson 2 Final Consonants	**Phoneme Manipulation:** Substitute the ending sound in words	Crossword Puzzles with Final Consonants Activity Pages 12–13			Write a list of school tools and furniture. Circle the ending letters. Then make a crossword puzzle with clues using eight of the words.
Lesson 3 Medial Consonants	**Phoneme Identity:** *yellow, jelly, wallet wagon, sugar, begin*	Word Boxes with Medial Consonants Activity Pages 14–15 Review Consonants Activity Page 16			Brainstorm lists of words that have the same middle sound. Write riddles about several of the words.
Lesson 4 Variant *c*	**Phoneme Identity:** *cat, cane, cow city, celery, cent*	Word Ladders with Variant *c* Activity Pages 17–18			Write a paragraph about a clown at a circus.
Lesson 5 Variant *g*	**Phoneme Identity:** *goat, gas, gum gym, giant, giraffe bridge, fudge, hedge*	Word Wall with Variant *g* Activity Pages 19–20			Write a paragraph about a giant who has a garden.
Lesson 6 Variant *s*	**Phoneme Identity:** *sun, sock, sail rose, cheese, choose tissue, sugar, sure*	Word Sort with Variant *s* Activity Pages 21–22 Review Variant *c, g,* and *s* Activity Page 23			Write a short story using the words *seal, rose,* and *tissue.*
Lesson 7 Story: "Cecil Sees Circles"			*circles, plays* Activity Page 24	Story Pages 25–28	

Unit 1: Consonants

Develop Phonemic Awareness

You may wish to review the letter sounds using these phonemic awareness techniques before students see the letters.

- **Phoneme Manipulation** Say a word and instruct children to substitute one sound for another sound. Example: *Listen to this word: net. Change /n/ to /p/.* (pet)
- **Phoneme Identity** As you introduce each letter, say the corresponding group of words below. Have children identify the sound that all words have in common. Then challenge children to brainstorm other words that have the same sound.

> Medial Consonants: yellow, jelly, wallet
> wagon, sugar, begin
>
> Variant *c*: cat, cane, cow
> city, celery, cent
>
> Variant *g*: goat, gas, gum
> gym, giant, giraffe
> bridge, fudge, hedge
>
> Variant *s*: sun, sock, sail
> rose, cheese, choose
> tissue, sugar, sure

Explore Phonics

Use these class activities to help children explore the letters and their sounds.

- **Word Building with Initial Consonants** Have partners write a word with a phonogram on paper. Invite children to take turns changing the first consonant to make a new word.
- **Crossword Puzzles with Final Consonants** Pair children and distribute Master 5 on page 153. Have partners take turns writing words that connect with an ending consonant. You may wish to have them number the words, write definitions or sentences, and redraw the puzzle with blank boxes to share with classmates.
- **Word Boxes with Medial Consonants** Using the grid from Master 4 on page 152, write 16 words that have a medial consonant. Copy the page and pair children. To play the game, players each choose a crayon. Have

children take turns reading a word and coloring the box if the word is read correctly. The player coloring the most boxes wins.

- **Word Ladders with Variant *c*** Write words that are spelled with *c*, including *cat* and *cent*, on index cards. Tape the cards with *cat* and *cent* along the bottom of a wall. Then pass out the remaining cards to children. Help each child read the word and tape the card above the word with the matching sound to form a "ladder."
- **Word Wall with Variant *g*** Establish a word wall in which children contribute words they hear or read that have a variant *g* sound. Have children write words that have the /g/ sound on green rectangles and words that have the /j/ sound on orange rectangles.
- **Word Sort with Variant *s*** Using the grid from Master 4 on page 152, write 16 words that are spelled with an *s*. Invite children to cut the boxes apart and sort them into groups with the /s/, /z/, or /sh/ sound.

Develop Vocabulary and Meaning

Letter Words

Variant *c*: Cecil, circles, clown, come

Variant *g*: along, goes, gym, having

Variant *s*: circles, is, looks, lots, plays, saw, see, sees, sun, sure, turns, ways

High-Frequency Words

a, all, at, be, can, do, he, in, it's, of, out, see, the, to, where, with, you

Story Words

around, dish, everywhere, found, fun, late, light, likes, night, remember, rim, today, very, when, wow

Vocabulary Words

circles, plays

The following activities will help prepare children for reading the unit story independently. Afterwards, children can complete the vocabulary exercise on page 24.

- **Circle Words** Cut out circles that are three different sizes. Write the high-frequency words on the largest circles, the letter words on the medium circles, and the story words on the smallest circles. Have children take turns tossing a beanbag on the circles and reading the words. Children are awarded one point for each word read from the smallest circles, two points for the medium circles, and three points for words read from the largest circles.

• **Explore Variant Letters** Write the letter words on individual cards. Introduce the words and discuss the sounds that the variant letters stand for. Then pass the cards out to children. Say a variant sound and have the children holding the cards with a word having that sound stand.

• **Homonyms** Explain that some words can have more than one meaning. Write *bat* on the chalkboard and draw a baseball bat and the flying animal underneath the word. Use both words in a sentence. Continue the explanation using the words *dish* and *light*.

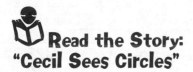

Read the Story: "Cecil Sees Circles"

Before Reading
Display the cover of the book and read the title. Invite children to page through the book to name the places they see circles. Then ask children to follow along in their books as you read the story.

During Reading
• **Model Fluency** As you read aloud the story, model the fluent reading skills of using a steady voice to read statements, a rising voice for questions, and an excited voice for exclamations.

• **Model Comprehension** You may wish to model how to identify the main idea by asking: *What is this story mostly about?*

After Reading
Have children find and read the words or phrases in the story that answer these questions:

What does Cecil see? (circles)

Who does Cecil see having fun? (clown)

Where does Cecil play with a ball? (gym)

What does Cecil do to show that he likes circles? (Answers will vary.)

Reread the Story: "Cecil Sees Circles"

• **Circle Reading** Have children sit in a circle as they read the story about Cecil who sees circles. Move around the circle, giving each child a chance to read a sentence. Read the story more than once, if necessary, to give everyone a turn.

• **Explore Rhyming Words** Reread the story and have children identify the pairs of rhyming words. Write the words on the chalkboard and challenge children to suggest other words that rhyme with them.

• **Fluent Reading** Have children turn to page 8. Point out the period, the question mark, and the exclamation points. Model the correct voice intonations for reading the sentences with each punctuation mark. Encourage partners to rehearse the sentences until they can read them fluently.

 **Connect the Story to Writing**

• **Continue the Story** Challenge children to write and illustrate a continuation of "Cecil Sees Circles" by telling other places that Cecil might see circles. Have children label their illustrations using the sentence frame *Cecil sees circles when* _____.

 **Support ESOL Learners**

Some non-English speakers may find it confusing that the letters *c, g,* and *s* have multiple sounds. Encourage children to sort cards with words or pictures whose names contain the sounds.

At Home

Encourage children to read "Cecil Sees Circles" with someone at home. Suggest that after reading the story, they look for circles at home and make a list of the places where circles can be found.

Beginning Consonant Sounds

Say each picture name. Write the consonant that stands for the **first** sound.

1	2	3	4

5	6	7	8

9	10	11	12

13	14	15	16

Hidden Picture with Beginning Consonant Sounds

Read each word. Use an orange crayon to color the parts that name an animal. What is hiding in the picture?

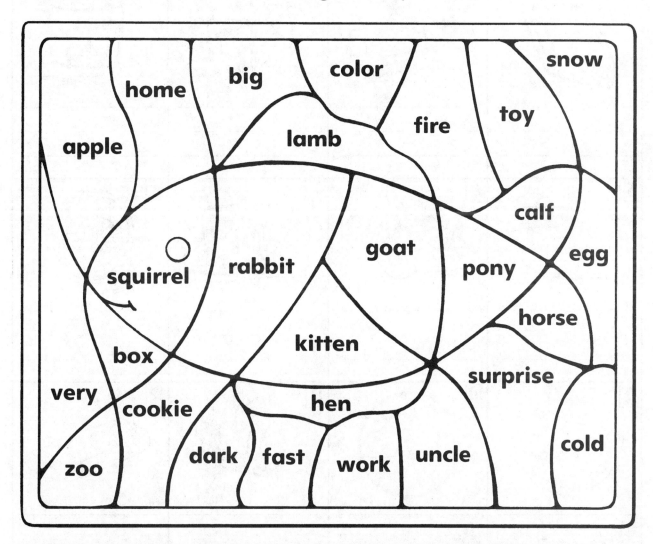

Write the names of the animals in ABC order.

_____

- -

_____

- -

_____

- -

_____

Ending Consonant Sounds

Say each picture name. Write the consonant that stands for the **last** sound.

1	2	3	4
5	6	7	8
9	10	11	12
13	14	15	16

Phonics, Second Grade SV 8862-5

Name _____ Date _____

Mystery Ending Consonant Sounds

Write the same consonant in each word to complete
the sentence.

1. A ca_____ sa_____ under a ha_____.

2. Loo_____ how Mom will coo_____ with mil_____.

3. The bu_____ stop_____ for ga_____.

4. That bi_____ fro_____ jumped into the lo_____.

5. Jim sai_____, "This foo_____ is goo_____ to eat!"

6. The he_____ had fu_____ i_____ the su_____.

Middle Consonant Sounds

Say each picture name. Write the consonant that stands for the **middle** sound.

1	2	3
ca __ el	wa __ on	bea __ er

4	5	6
li __ ard	fo __ es	ro __ in

7	8	9
pa __ er	sa __ ad	ca __ oe

10	11	12
ba __ on	gui __ ar	spi __ er

Puzzles with Middle Consonant Sounds

Look at each picture clue. Write a word from the box to complete each puzzle.

camel	lemon	river	robot	shovel	table

1.

2.

3.

4.

5.

6.

Phonics, Second Grade SV 8862-5

Review Consonant Sounds

Darken the circle beside the word that completes
each sentence. Then write the word on the line.

1

I went to the _____ .

○ too
○ zip
○ zoo

2

My _____ went, too.

○ pat
○ pal
○ pan

3

We rode on a _____ .

○ bug
○ bun
○ bus

4

The _____ was hot.

○ fun
○ run
○ sun

5

We saw a big _____ .

○ tiger
○ begin
○ sugar

6

We saw a _____ , too.

○ seat
○ seal
○ meal

7

It splashed in the _____ .

○ wagon
○ water
○ window

8

We got all _____ .

○ web
○ wet
○ well

Sounds of c

__cent   __cat

When **c** is before **e**, **i**, or **y**, it can stand for the **s** sound in **sun**. When **c** is before other letters, it stands for the **c** sound in **cat**.

Say the name of the first picture in each row. Circle the pictures that have the same **c** sound as the first picture.

__cent	cup	pencil	fence	cake
__cat	cap	city	can	mice
ra__ce	lace	cut	ice	car
__cymbals	cane	camel	celery	face

Rhyming Riddles with the Sounds of c

Read each clue. Think about the word in dark print. Write a word that rhymes with that word and begins with **c** or has **c** in the middle to solve the riddle. The first one is done for you.

1 What **hat** can an animal wear on its head?

$\boxed{A}$ _c_ _a_ _t_   _h_ _a_ _t_

2 What do you call a statue of frozen **mice**?

____ ____ ____ ____   _m_ _i_ _c_ _e_

3 What kind of bear takes a bath in a **tub**?

$\boxed{A}$ _t_ _u_ _b_   ____ ____ ____

4 What do you call a penny that is **bent**?

$\boxed{A}$ _b_ _e_ _n_ _t_   ____ ____ ____ ____

5 What does a **goat** wear to stay warm?

$\boxed{A}$ _g_ _o_ _a_ _t_   ____ ____ ____ ____

Sounds of g

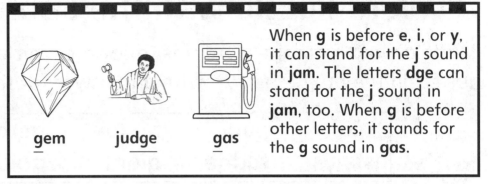

gem   judge   gas

When **g** is before **e**, **i**, or **y**, it can stand for the **j** sound in **jam**. The letters **dge** can stand for the **j** sound in **jam**, too. When **g** is before other letters, it stands for the **g** sound in **gas**.

Say the name of the first picture in each row. Circle the pictures that have the same **g** sound as the first picture.

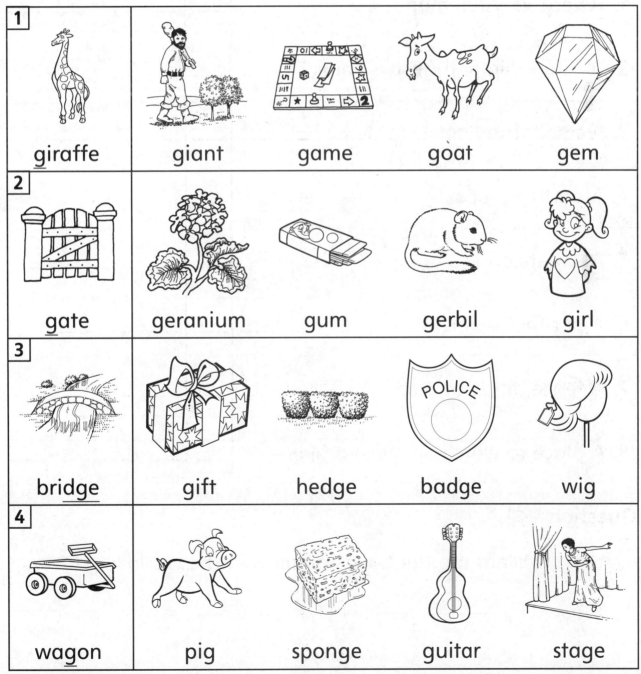

1 | giraffe | giant | game | goat | gem

2 | gate | geranium | gum | gerbil | girl

3 | bridge | gift | hedge | badge | wig

4 | wagon | pig | sponge | guitar | stage

Word Puzzle with the Sounds of g

Write a word from the word box to solve each clue. Then use the letters in the puzzle box to write an answer for the question.

pig	page	hedge	gerbil
stage	fudge	giant	goldfish

1. A very, very tall man   __ | __ | __ __ __

2. A farm animal that says "oink"   __ | __ | __

3. A small, furry pet   __ __ | __ | __ __

4. A part of a book   __ | __ | __ __

5. A sweet candy   __ | __ | __ __

6. A pet that swims   __ __ __ __ | __ | __ __

7. A fence made of plants   __ | __ | __ __

8. A place to watch actors in a play   __ | __ | __ __ __

Question

What are the tallest animals in the world?

__ __ __ __ __ __ __ __

Sounds of s

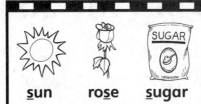

sun   rose   sugar

In **sun**, **s** stands for the **s** sound.
In **rose**, **s** stands for the **z** sound.
In **sugar**, **s** stands for the **sh** sound.

Say the name of the first picture in each row. Circle the pictures that have the same **s** sound as the first picture.

1				
s̲oap	bus	hos̲e	mask	toes

2				
mus̲ic	sock	fuse	seal	peas

3				
mis̲s̲ion	tissue	sugar	seed	cheese

4				
ga̲s̲	nose	vase	pies	dress

Name _____ Date _____

Hidden Picture with the Sounds of s

Read each word. Use a yellow crayon to color the parts in which **s** has the same sound as **sun**. What is hiding in the picture?

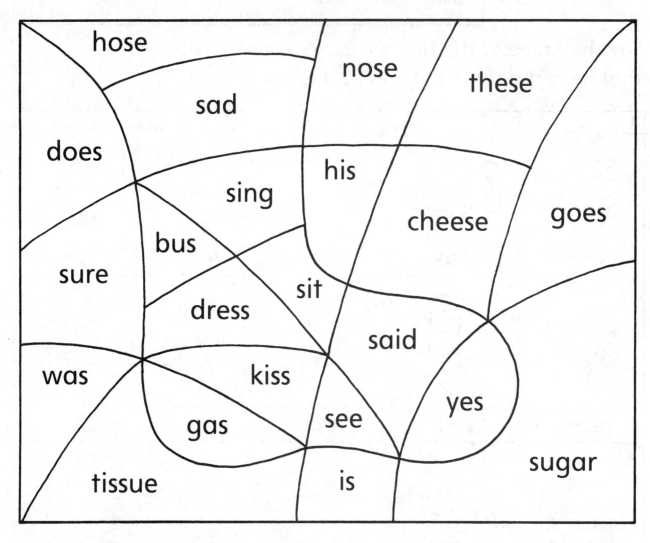

Write a sentence about what is hiding in the picture.

_____

_ _

_____

_ _

_____

_ _

_____

Unit 1: Variant *s*
Phonics, Second Grade SV 8862-5

Name _____ Date _____

Review the Sounds of c, g, and s

Darken the circle beside the word that completes each sentence. Then write the word on the line.

1

_____

The cat lives in the _____.

- ○ city
- ○ cent
- ○ cake

2

_____

The cat likes to chase little _____.

- ○ ice
- ○ nice
- ○ mice

3

_____

They run to hide in a small _____.

- ○ giant
- ○ gas
- ○ garden

4

_____

The cat looks in the _____.

- ○ fudge
- ○ hedge
- ○ cage

5

_____

Soon, the cat _____ looking.

- ○ sock
- ○ sun
- ○ stops

6

_____

He is _____ the little animals are gone.

- ○ sure
- ○ sugar
- ○ sudden

7 One mouse looks out from

_____

behind a _____.

- ○ nose
- ○ rose
- ○ goes

8

_____

"It is safe to eat the _____," the mouse said.

- ○ please
- ○ plays
- ○ peas

Vocabulary

Look at the pictures and read the word meanings. Then read the sentences. What does the word in dark print mean? Write the letter for the correct meaning of the word.

circles

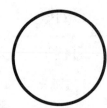 **a.** round shapes that have no corners or sides

 **b.** to draw or write a round shape

___ **1.** Cecil **circles** his answers on the test.

___ **2.** Cecil used a stick to make **circles** in the sand.

___ **3.** Bubbles look like little **circles**.

plays

 **a.** to have fun

 **b.** shows where people act

___ **4.** Sam acted in other **plays**.

___ **5.** Sam **plays** with his dog.

___ **6.** What kind of **plays** do you like to watch?

Cecil Sees Circles

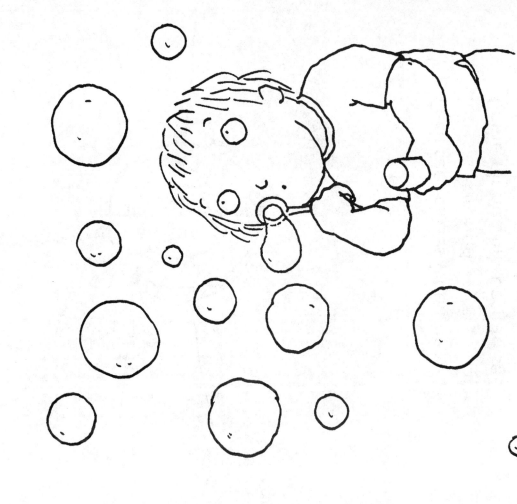

Cecil sees circles when he turns out the light!
Wow! Cecil sure saw lots of circles today.
Do you remember all of the ways?

8

Cecil sees circles when he
looks all around.
Come along with Cecil to see
where circles can be found.

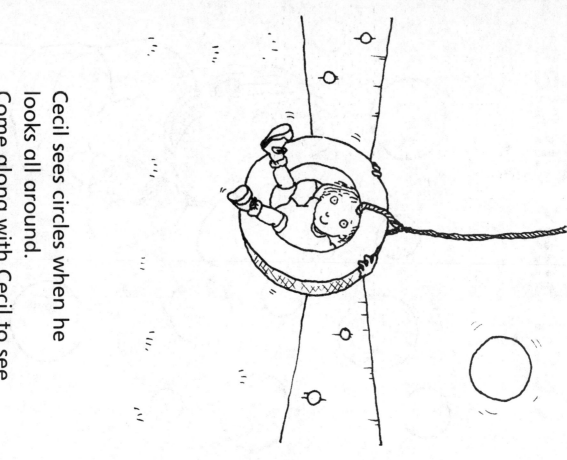

Cecil sees circles when it's
very late at night.

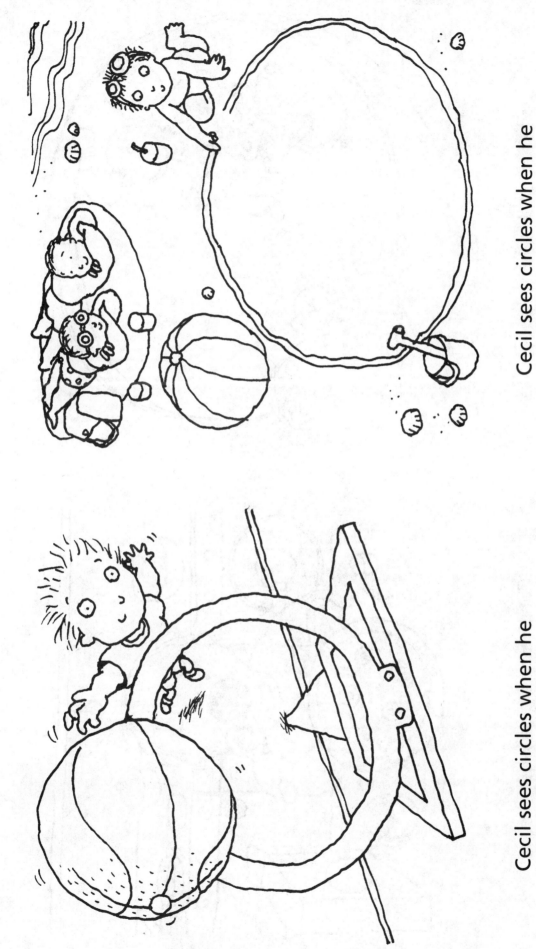

Cecil sees circles when he plays in the sun.

Cecil sees circles when he goes to the gym.

Cecil sees circles when a clown is having fun.

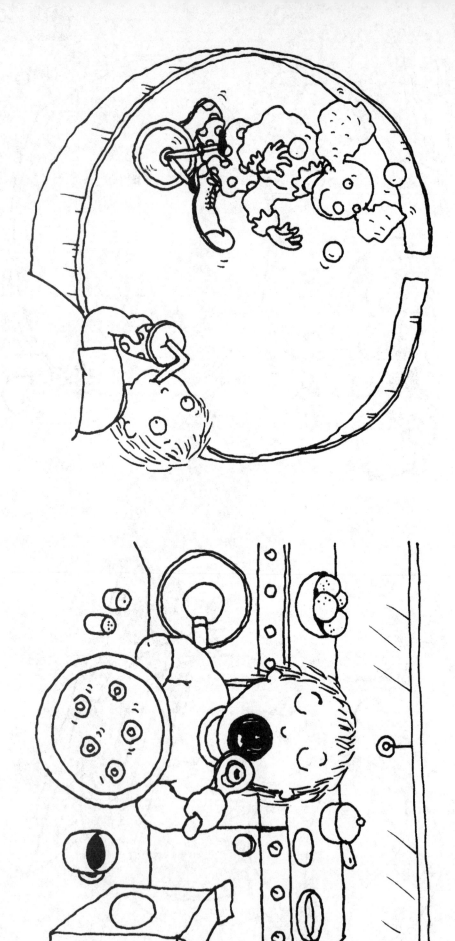

Cecil sees circles when he sees the dish rim.

Unit 2 Planner
Short Vowels

Lesson	Phonemic Awareness	Phonics	Vocabulary	Comprehension and Fluency	Writing
Lesson 1 **Short Vowel** *a*	**Phoneme Identity:** *apple, cat, gas* **Phoneme Segmentation:** *ax, pan, hand*	Word Hunt with Short *a* Activity Pages 32–33			Write silly sentences using words that have the short *a* sound.
Lesson 2 **Short Vowel** *o*	**Phoneme Identity:** *olives, frog, clock* **Phoneme Segmentation:** *box, pop, mop*	Word Wall with Short *o* Activity Pages 34–35			Write riddles whose answers have the short *o* sound.
Lesson 3 **Short Vowel** *i*	**Phoneme Identity:** *ink, chick, pin* **Phoneme Segmentation:** *bib, hid, zip*	Word Building with Short *i* Activity Pages 36–37 Review Short *a*, *o*, and *i* Activity Page 38			Write a paragraph telling about a time children win something. Challenge them to use as many words with the short *i* sound as they can.
Lesson 4 **Short Vowel** *u*	**Phoneme Identity:** *up, duck, bug* **Phoneme Segmentation:** *gum, bus, drum*	Flip Book with Short *u* Activity Pages 39–40			Brainstorm a list of words that rhyme with *bug*. Then write a paragraph about a bug using as many words on the list as possible.
Lesson 5 **Short Vowel** *e*	**Phoneme Identity:** *egg, nest, bell* **Phoneme Segmentation:** *bed, ten, desk*	Word Ladders with Short *e* Activity Pages 41–42 Review Short Vowels Activity Pages 43–45			Take a walk around the school building to find things whose names have a short *e* sound. Write the words in the Writer's Dictionary.
Lesson 6 **Story: "The Nest"**			*looks, picks, string, twigs, twists* Activity Page 46	Story Pages 47–50	

Unit 2: Short Vowels

Develop Phonemic Awareness

You may wish to introduce the short vowel sounds using these phonemic awareness techniques before students see the letters.

• **Phoneme Identity** As you introduce each letter, say the corresponding group of words below. Have children identify the sound that all words have in common. Then challenge children to brainstorm other words that begin with the same sound.

Short *a*: apple, cat, gas
Short *o*: olives, frog, clock
Short *i*: ink, chick, pin
Short *u*: up, duck, bug
Short *e*: egg, nest, bell

• **Phoneme Segmentation** Tell children that you will sound out a word. Have them count the sounds they hear. Then have children repeat the phonemes and identify the word. Next, repeat the segmented word and have children write it in their Writer's Dictionary.

Short *a*: ax, pan, hand
Short *o*: box, pop, mop
Short *i*: bib, hid, zip
Short *u*: gum, bus, drum
Short *e*: bed, ten, desk

Explore Phonics

Use these class activities to help children explore each short vowel letter and sound.

• **Word Hunt with Short a** Invite partners to go on a sound hunt using the grid from Master 4 on page 152. Ask partners to look for pictures or words whose names have the short *a* sound. Challenge children to find as many words as they can to write on the grid.

• **Word Wall with Short o** Establish a word wall in which children contribute words they hear or read that have a short *o* sound.

• **Word Building with Short i** Have partners write a word with a short *i* sound on paper. Invite children to take turns changing one consonant to make a new word.

• **Flip Book with Short u** Invite children to make a flip book with a phonogram that has the short *u* sound using Master 3 on page 151. Challenge children to choose one word from their book and use it in a sentence.

• **Word Ladders with Short e** Challenge children to write words that have a short *e* phonogram on index cards. Have them sort and then tape the cards to the appropriate "ladder."

Develop Vocabulary and Meaning

Letter Words
Short *a*: grass, has
Short *o*: moss, on
Short *i*: in, into, is, picks, sings, sits, string, twigs, twins, twists
Short *u*: up
Short *e*: eggs, nest

High-Frequency Words
a, all, and, her, in, is, looks, more, now, of, on, one, she, some, the, there

Story Words
again, baby, bird, flies, lays, made, mother, together, tree, tweet, two

Vocabulary Words
looks, picks, string, twigs, twists

The following activities will help prepare children for reading the unit story independently. Afterwards, children can complete the vocabulary exercise on page 46.

• **Word Riddles** Write the words from the story that have short vowel sounds on index cards. Pass them out to children. Ask questions about one of the words, such as: *I begin like* sock, *but rhyme with* kings. *What am I?* (sings) Have the child holding the card that answers the riddle stand. Help the child read the card out loud.

• **Nest Words** Draw five nests on mural paper. Label each nest with *a, o, i, u,* or *e.* Using the cards from the activity above, show the cards to children. Invite a volunteer to read the word and tape the card to the nest that shows the corresponding letter.

- **Synonyms** Remind children that some words can have the same or almost the same meaning. Challenge children to name synonyms for the following words: *big (large), happy (glad), jump (hop), laugh (giggle).*

Read the Story: "The Nest"

Before Reading

Display the cover of the book and read the title. Invite children to page through the book to see what the bird uses to make a nest. Then ask children to follow along in their books as you read the story.

During Reading

- **Model Fluency** As you read aloud the story, model the fluent reading skills of reading exclamatory sentences with excitement and pausing for commas in a series.
- **Model Comprehension** You may wish to model how to identify the story plot by drawing a simple flow chart and helping children list the sequence of events as they read along.

After Reading

Have children find and read the words or phrases in the story that answer these questions:

What does the bird make? (nest)

What does the bird use to make the nest? (grass, moss, twigs, string)

Why did the bird make the nest? (to lay eggs)

How is a bird's nest like your house? (Answers will vary.)

Reread the Story: "The Nest"

- **Retell the Story** Invite children to tell what happens in the story in their own words. Encourage them to tell the story as a narrative, using picture details to help them recognize the sequence of events.

- **Develop Oral Language** Have pairs of children act out the story. They can pretend to be the birds. Encourage them to explain what they are doing as they act out their parts.
- **Fluent Reading** Have children turn to page 6. Model how to read exclamatory sentences with excitement and serial commas with appropriate speed. Encourage partners to rehearse the sentences until they can read them fluently.

Connect the Story to Writing

- **Writing Directions** Ask children to write directions telling how a bird makes a nest. Encourage them to use time order words in their writing.
- **Continue the Story** Invite children to tell what the birds in the story will do next. Have children draw a picture to go along with their writing.

Support ESOL Learners

Children whose native language is Italian may have trouble hearing or saying the short *a* sound. Children whose native language is Greek, Italian, or Japanese may have trouble hearing or saying the short *i* sound. Children whose native language is Urdu may have trouble hearing or saying the short *e* sound.

At Home

Encourage children to read "The Nest" with someone at home. Suggest that they spend some time outside watching birds to see if they can spot birds carrying things in their beaks. Encourage children to make a list of those things and bring it to school to share with the class.

Short Vowel a

Apple and **cat** have the short **a** sound.

Say each picture name. Then write **a** if you hear the short **a** sound.

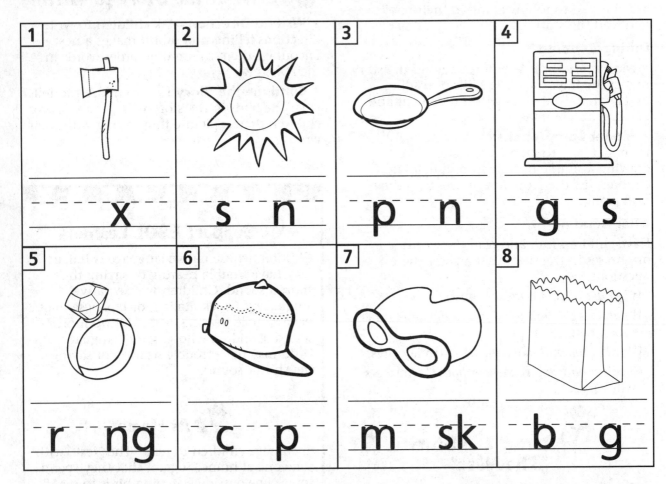

1	2	3	4
x	s n	p n	g s

5	6	7	8
r ng	c p	m sk	b g

Write a sentence about the picture.

_____
_____
_____
_____

Maze with Short Vowel a

Read each word. Color the box if the word has the short **a** sound. Then follow the path to find what the cat did.

Start

hat	ant	can	fan
box	sun	fish	ax
net	van	cap	bat
doll	hand	bus	bird

Name _____ Date _____

Short Vowel o

Olives and frog have the short o sound.

Say each picture name. Then write **o** if you hear the
short **o** sound.

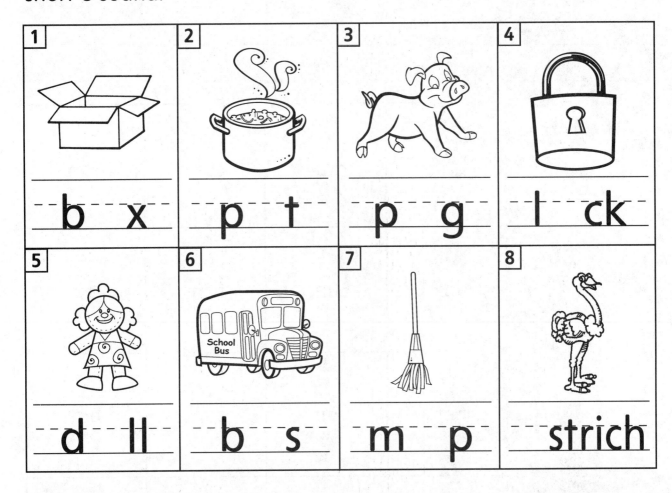

1	2	3	4
b __ x	p __ t	p __ g	l __ ck

5	6	7	8
d __ ll	b __ s	m __ p	__ strich

Write a sentence about the picture.

_____

_____

_____

_____

Phonics, Second Grade SV 8862-5

Riddles with Short Vowel o

Write a word from the box to answer each riddle.

clock	cot	doll	pop	sock	top

1. I have a toe and a heel, but I am not part of your body. What am I?

_____

2. I have eyes, but I cannot see. I have a nose, but I cannot smell. What am I?

_____

3. I have hands, but I cannot hold things. I have a face, but I do not have a nose, eyes, or mouth. What am I?

_____

4. I have legs to stand on, but people lay down on me. What am I?

_____

5. I can be something to drink. I can also be a loud noise. What am I?

_____

6. My name says I am up high, but I really spin low on the ground. What am I?

_____

Short Vowel i

Ink and **chick** have the short i sound.

Say each picture name. Then write **i** if you hear the
short **i** sound.

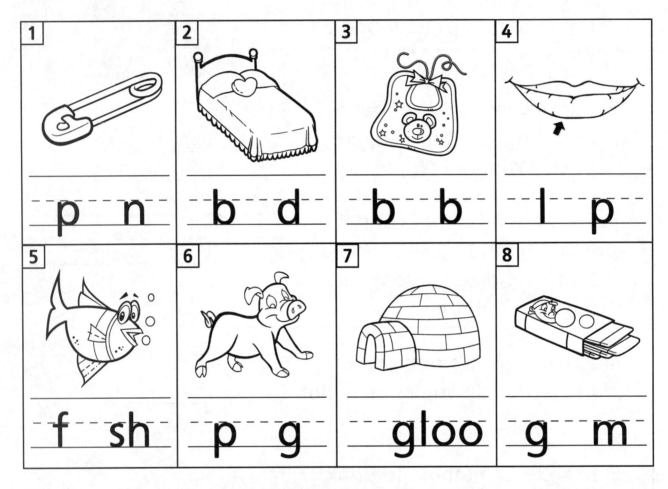

1	2	3	4
p ___ n	b ___ d	b ___ b	l ___ p

5	6	7	8
f ___ sh	p ___ g	gloo ___	g ___ m

Write a sentence about the picture.

_____
- - - - - - - - - - - - -
_____
- - - - - - - - - - - - -
_____

Rhyming Words with Short Vowel i

Read the words in each fish. Color the parts of the fish that have the rhyming words.

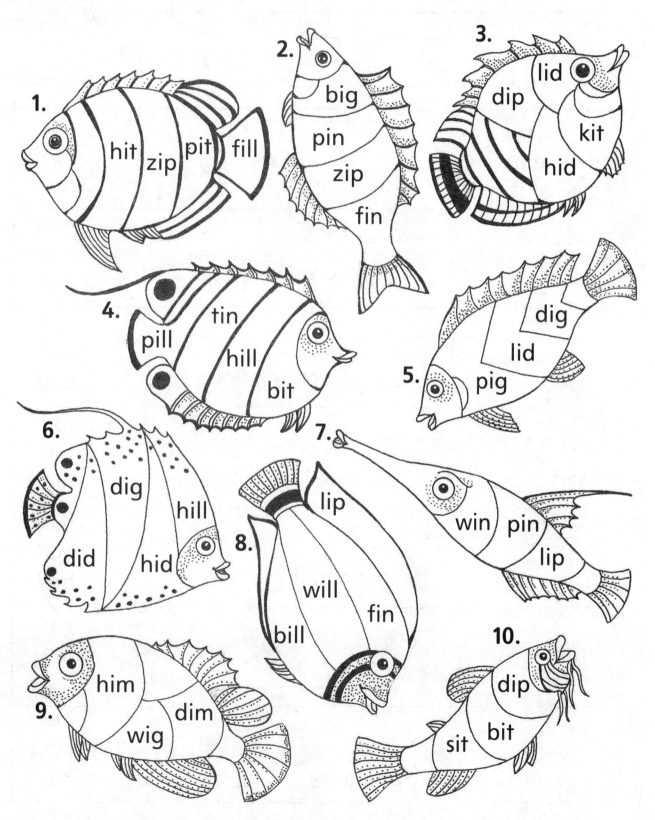

1. hit zip pit fill

2. big pin zip fin

3. lid dip kit hid

4. tin pill hill bit

5. dig lid pig

6. dig hill did hid

7. win pin lip

8. lip will fin bill

9. him dim wig

10. dip bit sit

Name ______________________ Date ______________

Review Short Vowels a, o, and i

Darken the circle beside the word that completes each sentence. Then write the word on the line.

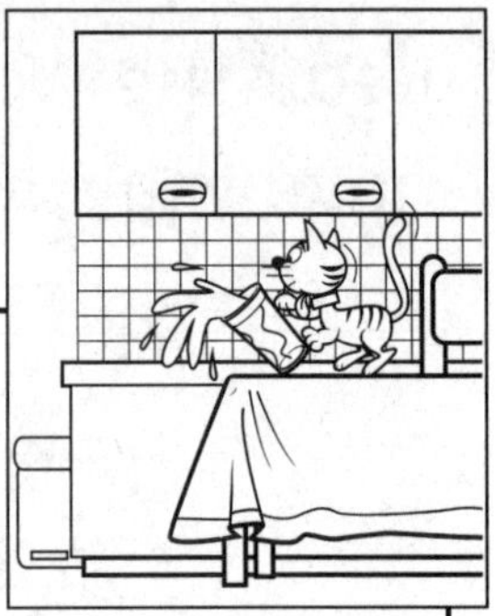

1. Max had a pet ______________.
   - ○ cot
   - ○ cat
   - ○ cut

2. It jumped on ______________ of the kitchen table.
   - ○ tap
   - ○ tip
   - ○ top

3. Some ______________ spilled from a cup.
   - ○ milk
   - ○ man
   - ○ mom

4. It began to ______________ on the floor.
   - ○ doll
   - ○ dad
   - ○ drip

5. The pet ______________ out of the room.
   - ○ rot
   - ○ rip
   - ○ ran

6. It ______________ under a bed.
   - ○ hid
   - ○ had
   - ○ hot

7. Max saw that he had a ______________ to do.
   - ○ jib
   - ○ job
   - ○ jab

8. Max cleaned the floor with a ______________.
   - ○ mop
   - ○ map
   - ○ mitt

Short Vowel u

Up and **duck** have the short **u** sound.

Say each picture name. Then write **u** if you hear the short **u** sound.

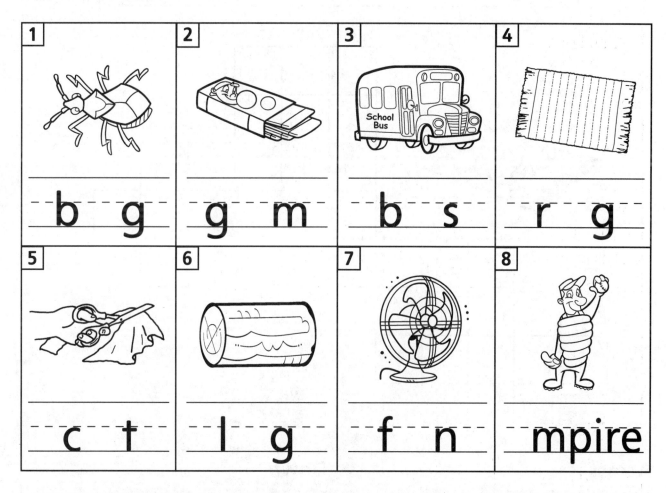

1	2	3	4
b __ g	g __ m	b __ s	r __ g
5	6	7	8
c __ t	l __ g	f __ n	__ mpire

Write a sentence about the picture.

_____

_____

_____

_____

Crossword Puzzle with Short Vowel **u**

Read each clue. Write a word from the box to complete the puzzle.

bug	duck	drum	gum	up
mug	skunk	truck	tub	

Across

1. Something that you can wash in

3. A candy that can be chewed

5. The opposite of down

6. An animal that has wings and a bill

7. A black and white animal

Down

1. Something that you can ride in

2. A small animal with a hard shell

4. Something that you can drink from

6. A kind of instrument that you can hit

Short Vowel e

Egg and **nest** have the short **e** sound.

Say each picture name. Then write **e** if you hear the short **e** sound.

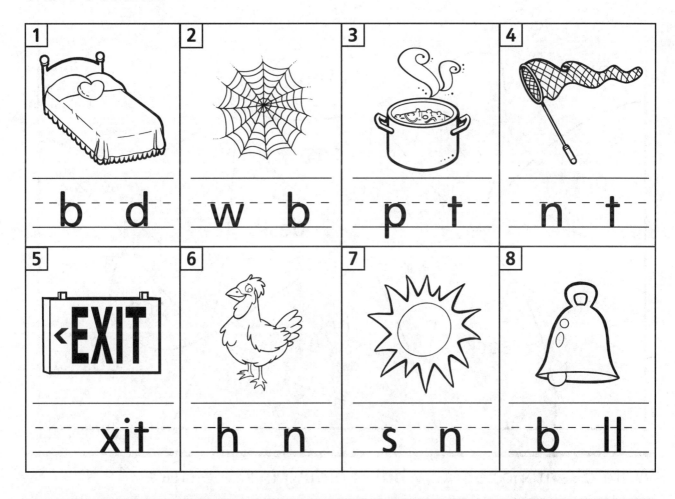

1	2	3	4
b ___ d	w ___ b	p ___ t	n ___ t

5	6	7	8
___ xit	h ___ n	s ___ n	b ___ ll

Write a sentence about the picture.

_____

- - - - - - - - - - - - - - - -

_____

- - - - - - - - - - - - - - - -

_____

Hidden Picture with Short Vowel e

Read each word. Use a green crayon to color the parts in which the word has a short **e** sound. What is hiding in the picture?

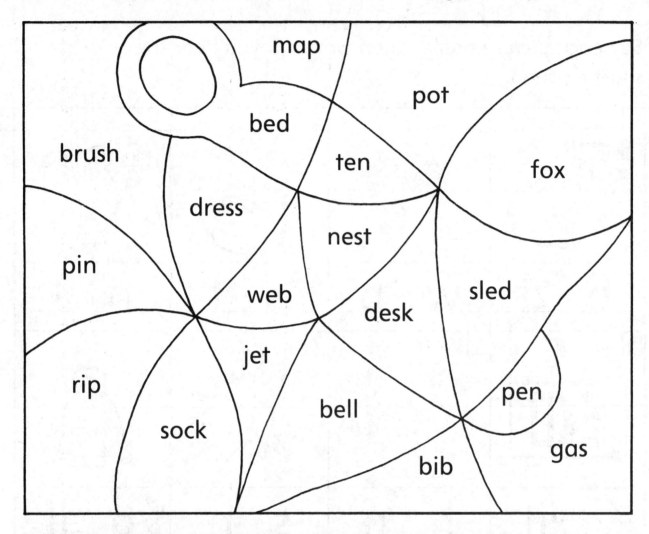

Write a sentence about what is hiding in the picture.

_____

- -

_____

- -

_____

- -

Name _____ Date _____

Review Short Vowels **u** and **e**

Darken the circle beside the word that completes each sentence. Then write the word on the line.

1 _____

_____ little pigs went out to play.

- ○ Tug
- ○ Ten
- ○ Tub

2 They ran, hopped, and _____.

- ○ jumped
- ○ jelly
- ○ jets

3 One pig fell into a _____ puddle.

- ○ men
- ○ mud
- ○ mug

4 The _____ of the pigs hopped into the puddle, too.

- ○ nest
- ○ pest
- ○ rest

5 It got all over their _____.

- ○ legs
- ○ lets
- ○ less

6 Soon the little pigs _____ home.

- ○ west
- ○ well
- ○ went

7 "What a _____!" said Mother Pig.

- ○ less
- ○ mess
- ○ dress

8 Mother Pig filled a _____ with hot water.

- ○ tub
- ○ tent
- ○ test

Word Find for Short Vowels

Read the words in the box. Find each word in the puzzle and circle it. The words go across and down.

bit
hat
hop
man
pen
pig
red
rod
sun

a	b	f	d	g	h	o	p
r	r	e	d	x	r	z	u	e
y	s	p	m	k	r	i	n
c	d	h	a	t	f	c	h
x	s	z	n	j	b	i	t
q	u	t	l	r	t	p	o
p	n	h	l	e	n	i	h
o	y	c	p	b	t	g	u
b	m	r	o	d	n	e	s

Write a rhyming word for each word.

1. hop

2. man

3. pig

4. hat

5. pen

6. bit

7. red

8. sun

9. rod

www.svschoolsupply.com

© Harcourt Achieve Inc.

Unit 2: Review Short Vowels
Phonics, Second Grade SV 8862-5

Name _____ Date _____

Review Short Vowels

Darken the circle beside the word that completes each sentence. Then write the word on the line.

1
_____

Jen has a little pet _____.

○ pig
○ peg
○ rug

2
_____

It likes to _____.

○ dig
○ wig
○ big

3
_____

The pet gets in the _____.

○ mug
○ mad
○ mud

4
_____

Jen gets out a _____.

○ rub
○ tub
○ sub

5
_____

She fills it with _____ water.

○ hot
○ hat
○ hit

6
_____

Then the pet gets a _____.

○ math
○ bath
○ path

7
_____

The pet likes to get _____.

○ net
○ let
○ wet

8
_____

Jen dries it with a clean _____.

○ sag
○ rag
○ wag

www.svschoolsupply.com
© Harcourt Achieve Inc.

Unit 2: Review Short Vowels
Phonics, Second Grade SV 8862-5

Vocabulary

Read each word. Write the letters of the secret code to find the word that means the same or almost the same.

a	b	c	d	e	f	g	h	i	j	k	l	m
1	2	3	4	5	6	7	8	9	10	11	12	13

n	o	p	q	r	s	t	u	v	w	x	y	z
14	15	16	17	18	19	20	21	22	23	24	25	26

1. sees
$$\overline{}\ \overline{}\ \overline{}\ \overline{}\ \overline{}$$
12   15   15   11   19

2. wrings
$$\overline{}\ \overline{}\ \overline{}\ \overline{}\ \overline{}\ \overline{}$$
20   23   9   19   20   19

3. chooses
$$\overline{}\ \overline{}\ \overline{}\ \overline{}\ \overline{}$$
16   9   3   11   19

4. sticks
$$\overline{}\ \overline{}\ \overline{}\ \overline{}\ \overline{}$$
20   23   9   7   19

5. yarn
$$\overline{}\ \overline{}\ \overline{}\ \overline{}\ \overline{}\ \overline{}$$
19   20   18   9   14   7

The Nest

"Tweet! Tweet! Tweet!" sings mother bird again.
Now there is one more baby bird—twins!

Mother bird picks up some twigs.
She picks up some grass.

Mother bird looks in the nest.
There is one baby bird!

She picks up some moss.
She picks up some string.

Mother bird sits on the nest made of twigs,
grass, moss, and string.
"Tweet! Tweet! Tweet!" sings mother bird.

Mother bird flies up into a tree.
She twists the twigs, the grass, the moss,
and the string all together.

Mother bird has made a nest!
She lays two eggs in the nest.

Unit 3 Planner
Long Vowels

Lesson	Phonemic Awareness	Phonics	Vocabulary	Comprehension and Fluency	Writing
Lesson 1 Long Vowel *a*	**Phoneme Identity:** *ape, cane, mail* **Phoneme Segmentation:** *jay, cape, train*	Word Boxes with Long *a* Activity Pages 54–56			Write a letter that could be mailed to a friend or family member. Decorate the page to look like stationery.
Lesson 2 Long Vowel *o*	**Phoneme Identity:** *bone, coat, rose* **Phoneme Segmentation:** *mole, toad, bowl*	Word Building with Long *o* Activity Pages 57–59			Write silly sentences using words that have the long *o* sound.
Lesson 3 Long Vowel *i*	**Phoneme Identity:** *mice, bike, five* **Phoneme Segmentation:** *tie, nine, nice*	Crossword Puzzles with Long *i* Activity Pages 60–62 Review Long *a, o,* and *i* Activity Page 63			Write a store advertisement about a special price if people buy five ties.
Lesson 4 Long Vowel *u*	**Phoneme Identity:** *tube, glue, fuse* **Phoneme Segmentation:** *cute, mule, dune*	Word Wheel with Long *u* Activity Pages 64–65			Write a new song to a familiar tune, such as "Are You Sleeping?" Have children try to include words that have a long *u* sound.
Lesson 5 Long Vowel *e*	**Phoneme Identity:** *leaf, jeep, team* **Phoneme Segmentation:** *bee, seal, tree*	Flip Book with Long *e* Activity Pages 66–67 Review Long Vowels Activity Pages 68–69			Take a walk around the school building or on a trail to find things whose names have a long *e* sound. Write the words in the Writer's Dictionary.
Lesson 6 Story: "Squiggles"			*its, it's, sea, see, to, two* Activity Page 70	Story Pages 71–74	

© Harcourt Achieve Inc.

51

Unit 3: Planner
Phonics, Second Grade SV 8862-5

🐛 Develop Phonemic Awareness

You may wish to introduce the long vowel sounds using these phonemic awareness techniques before introducing them to children.

• **Phoneme Identity** As you introduce each long vowel, say the corresponding group of words below. Have children identify the sound that all words have in common. Then challenge children to brainstorm other words that contain the same sound.

Long *a*: ape, cane, mail
Long *o*: bone, coat, rose
Long *i*: mice, bike, five
Long *u*: tube, glue, fuse
Long *e*: leaf, jeep, team

• **Phoneme Segmentation** Tell children that you will sound out a word. Have them count the sounds they hear. Then have children repeat the phonemes and identify the word. Next, repeat the segmented word and have children write it in their Writer's Dictionary.

Long *a*: jay, cape, train
Long *o*: mole, toad, bowl
Long *i*: tie, nine, nice
Long *u*: cute, mule, dune
Long *e*: bee, seal, tree

🔤 Explore Phonics

Use these class activities to help children explore each long vowel letter and sound.

• **Word Boxes with Long a** Using the grid from Master 4 on page 152, write 16 words that have the long *a* sound. Copy the page and pair children. To play the game, players each choose a crayon. Have children take turns reading a word and coloring the box if the word is read correctly. The player coloring the most boxes wins.

• **Word Building with Long o** Help children make a step book using Master 2 on page 150. Have them write a word with a long *o* phonogram on the top page. On each tab, ask children to write instructions for changing one letter to form a new word. The new word is written above each instruction so it is hidden. For example, children write *boat* on the top page. The first tab will read "Change *b*

to *c*." The word *coat* is hidden above the instructions. The second tab will read "Change *c* to *g*." The word *goat* is hidden above this instruction, and so on.

• **Crossword Puzzles with Long i** Pair children and distribute Master 5 on page 153. Have partners take turns writing words that have the long *i* sound and spelling patterns to form a crossword puzzle. You may wish to have them number the words, write definitions or sentences, and redraw the puzzle with blank boxes to share with classmates.

• **Word Wheel with Long u** Invite children to make a word wheel using Master 1 on page 149. Help them write a phonogram with the long *u* sound on the larger wheel and letters that make words using the phonogram on the smaller wheel. Pair children and invite them to exchange the wheels and read the words.

• **Flip Book with Long e** Invite children to make a flip book with a phonogram that has the long *e* sound using Master 3 on page 151. Challenge children to choose one word from their book and use it in a sentence.

📖 Develop Vocabulary and Meaning

Letter Words

Long *a*: make, snake, tail
Long *o*: floating, stones
Long *i*: like, nice, spider, stripes
Long *u*: cute, mule
Long *e*: beak, green, me, sea, see

High-Frequency Words

a, and, are, can, do, from, in, is, its, it's, more, on, some, the, they, this, to, with, you

Story Words

back, black, ears, fish, ground, hen, imagination, its, long, round, skunk, snail, spots, squiggle, swirl, thin, things, two

Vocabulary Words

its, it's, sea, see, to, two

The following activities will help prepare children for reading the unit story independently. Afterwards, children can complete the vocabulary exercise on page 70.

- **Rhyming Words** Review the letter and story words in advance and choose a rhyming word for each. Then write a rhyming word on the chalkboard for one of those words. Have children find and read the rhyming word in the story aloud.
- **Listen for Long Vowel Sounds** Read the words used in the activity above in any order. Have children raise their hand if they hear a long vowel sound.
- **Homophones** Explain to children that homophones are words that sound alike, but they have different spellings and meanings. Write *to, two,* and *too* on the chalkboard and review their meanings. Then use each in a sentence.

 Read the Story: "Squiggles"

Before Reading

Display the cover of the book and read the title. Discuss what "squiggles" are. As children page through the book, explain that the pictures show squiggles that are not completed. Have them predict what the squiggles will become.

During Reading

- **Model Fluency** As you read aloud the story, model the fluent reading skills of reading questions and reading sentences with line breaks.
- **Model Comprehension** Encourage children to listen for details as you read the story. Pause after reading each page and invite children to finish the squiggles to reflect the information in the story.

After Reading

Have children find and read the words or phrases in the story that answer these questions:

What was the animal that was on the ground? (snake)

What was the round squiggle? (stone)

What was the animal with cute ears and a long tail? (mule)

How did the boy use his imagination? (Answers will vary.)

 Reread the Story: "Squiggles"

- **Reread the Story** Reread the story together and make a list of the things made from the squiggles. Have children identify the ones whose names have a long vowel sound.
- **Follow the Directions** Provide an easel, chart paper, and markers. Read aloud each direction in the story and have volunteers take turns drawing what the text says on the chart paper.
- **Fluent Reading** Have children turn to page 6. Model how to read sentences with line breaks and questions. Encourage children to practice reading the sentences until they can read them fluently.

 Connect the Story to Writing

- **Create a New Page** Invite children to make their own squiggles to represent objects. Have children identify their squiggles by writing sentences about them that follow the sentence pattern of the story: *This squiggle is a _____.* Encourage children to show their squiggles and read their lines to the rest of the class. Challenge the class to compose a second rhyming line.

Support ESOL Learners

Children whose native language is French, Urdu, or Vietnamese may have trouble hearing or saying the long *a* and *e* sounds. Children whose native language is Greek may have trouble hearing or saying the long *e* sound. Children whose native language is Chinese or Korean may have trouble hearing or saying the long *o* and *u* sounds.

At Home

Encourage children to read "Squiggles" with someone at home. After reading, suggest they take turns drawing a squiggle and guessing what shape the outline could represent.

Name _____ Date _____

Long Vowel a

Rake has the long **a** sound. The letters **a_e** can stand for the long **a** sound.

Write **a** and **e** under each picture that has the long **a** sound.

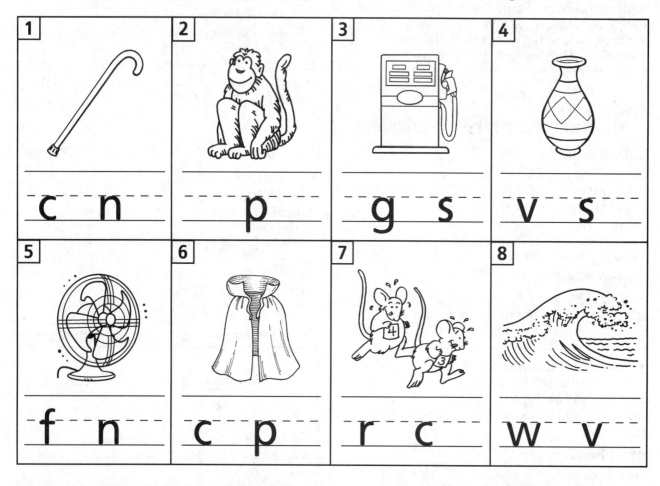

1 c ___ n

2 p ___

3 g ___ s

4 v ___ s

5 f ___ n

6 c ___ p

7 r ___ c

8 w ___ v

Write a sentence about the picture.

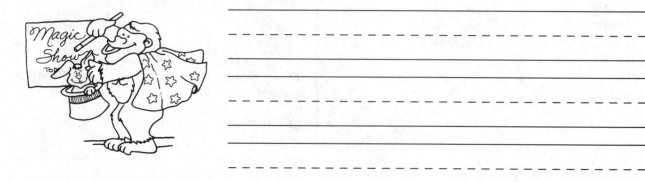

_____

_____

_____

_____

_____

_____

Long Vowel a

Quail and **hay** have the long **a** sound. The letters **ai** and **ay** can stand for the long **a** sound.

Circle the word that names each picture. Then write the word.

1. say
    sail
    save

2. nail
    nap
    name

3. pace
    pail
    pay

4. trade
    train
    tray

5. rain
    rake
    ray

6. jar
    jay
    jail

Write a sentence about the picture.

Rhyming Riddles with Long Vowel a

Read each clue. Think about the word in dark print. Write a word that rhymes with that word and has the long **a** sound to solve the riddle. The first one is done for you.

1 What do you call a rocket **race** to the moon?

A s p a c e   r a c e

2 What do you call a **cape** that is purple?

A __ __ __ __   c a p e

3 What do you call a **day** that a worker gets money?

A __ __ __   d a y

4 What do you call a bucket full of **nails**?

A n a i l   __ __ __ __

5 What do you call a sunny **day**?

A __ __ __   d a y

Long Vowel o

Rose has the long **o** sound. The letters **o_e** can stand for the long **o** sound.

Write **o** and **e** under each picture that has the long **o** sound.

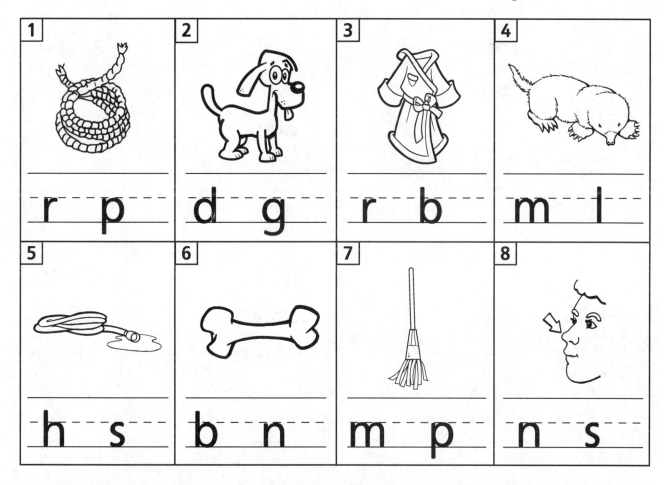

1	2	3	4
r ___ ___ p	d ___ ___ g	r ___ ___ b	m ___ ___ l

5	6	7	8
h ___ ___ s	b ___ ___ n	m ___ ___ p	n ___ ___ s

Write a sentence about the picture.

_____

- - - - - - - - - - - - - - - -

_____

- - - - - - - - - - - - - - - -

_____

Long Vowel o

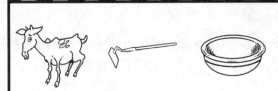

Goat, **hoe**, and **bowl** have the long **o** sound. The letters **oa**, **oe**, and **ow** can stand for the long **o** sound.

Circle the word that names each picture. Then write the word.

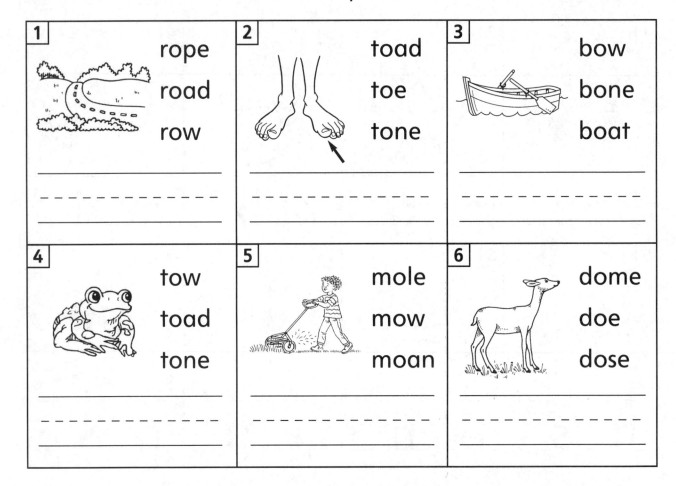

1

rope
road
row

_____

2

toad
toe
tone

_____

3

bow
bone
boat

_____

4

tow
toad
tone

_____

5

mole
mow
moan

_____

6

dome
doe
dose

_____

Write a sentence about the picture.

_____

_____

_____

_____

_____

Name _____ Date _____

Word Puzzles with Long Vowel o

Read the clues for each puzzle. Use rhyming words from the box to complete the puzzles.

1. A tool for the garden
2. A part of the foot

h		
i		
t		

hoe	pole
hole	nose
joke	rose
low	row
poke	toe

3. A funny story
4. To push with a finger

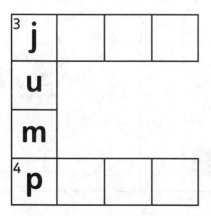

5. Something you dig
6. A long stick

7. A flower
8. A face part

9. A straight line of things
10. Not high

www.svschoolsupply.com
© Harcourt Achieve Inc.

Unit 3: Long Vowel o
Phonics, Second Grade SV 8862-5

Long Vowel i

Mice has the long i sound. The letters i_e can stand for the long i sound.

Write i and e under each picture that has the long i sound.

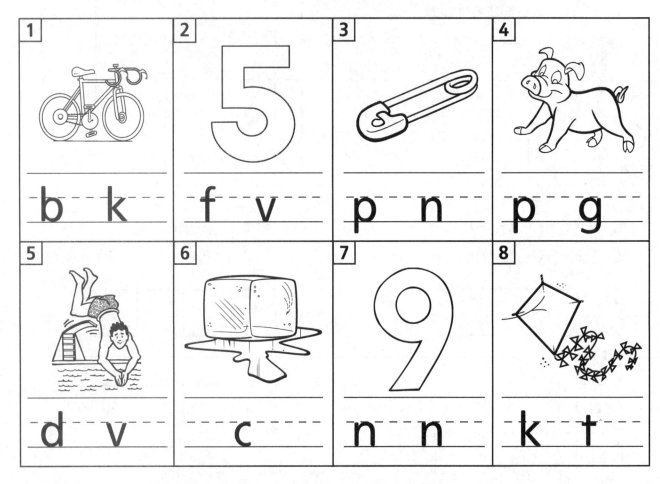

1. b ___ k
2. f ___ v
3. p ___ n
4. p ___ g
5. d ___ v
6. c ___
7. n ___ n
8. k ___ t

Write a sentence about the picture.

_____
_____
_____
_____
_____
_____

Long Vowel i

Pie and **five** have the long i sound. The letters **ie** and **i_e** can stand for the long i sound.

Circle the word that names each picture. Then write the word.

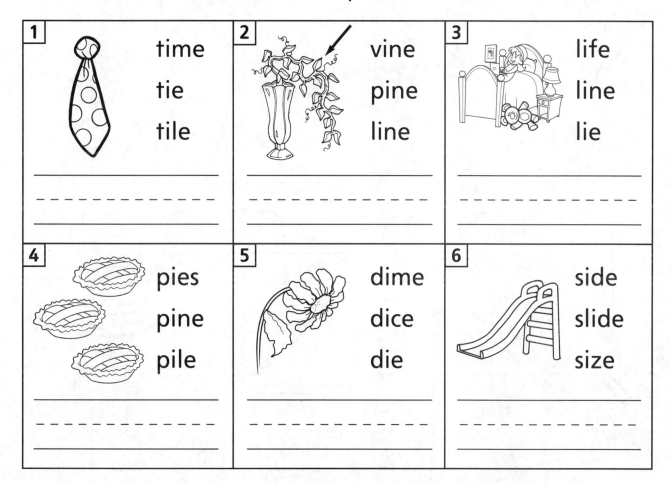

1

time

tie

tile

_____

- - - - - - - - - - - - - - -

2

vine

pine

line

_____

- - - - - - - - - - - - - - -

3

life

line

lie

_____

- - - - - - - - - - - - - - -

4

pies

pine

pile

_____

- - - - - - - - - - - - - - -

5

dime

dice

die

_____

- - - - - - - - - - - - - - -

6

side

slide

size

_____

- - - - - - - - - - - - - - -

Write a sentence about the picture.

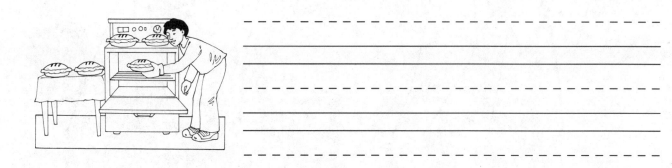

_____

- - - - - - - - - - - - - - -

_____

- - - - - - - - - - - - - - -

_____

Rhyming Words with Long Vowel i

Read the words on each kite. Color the kites if all the words rhyme.

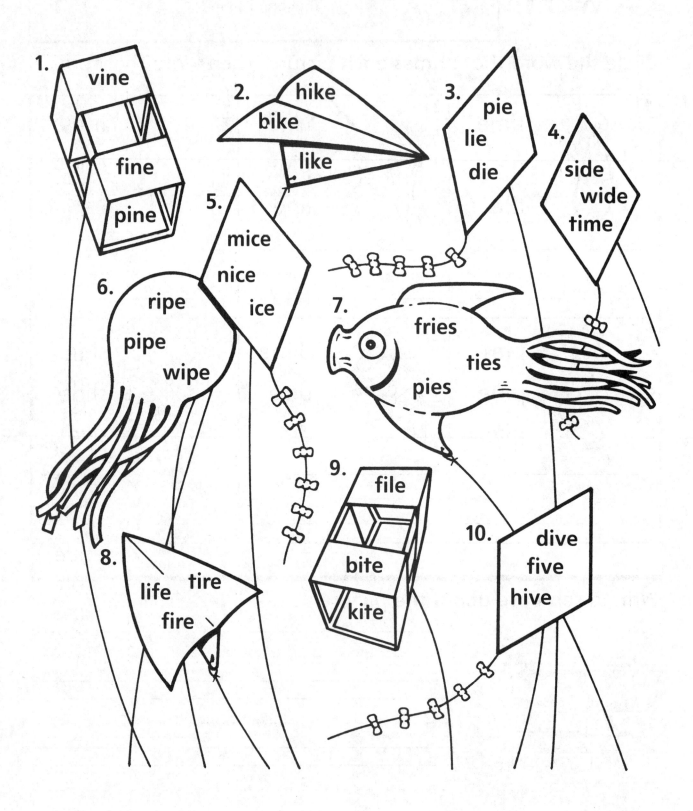

1. vine / fine / pine

2. hike / bike / like

3. pie / lie / die

4. side / wide / time

5. mice / nice / ice

6. ripe / pipe / wipe

7. fries / ties / pies

8. life / tire / fire

9. file / bite / kite

10. dive / five / hive

Name _____ Date _____

Review Long Vowels **a**, **o**, and **i**

Darken the circle beside the word that completes each sentence. Then write the word on the line.

1
Mom has a garden on the _____
of the house.

- ◯ sail
- ◯ side
- ◯ soap

2
Mom uses a _____ to dig in
the garden.

- ◯ hay
- ◯ hide
- ◯ hoe

3
She uses a _____ to smooth out
the dirt.

- ◯ rake
- ◯ road
- ◯ robe

4
Mom grows _____ in her garden.

- ◯ roses
- ◯ rays
- ◯ rides

5
She has a _____ of berries in her
garden, too.

- ◯ rain
- ◯ rise
- ◯ row

6
We pick the berries when they are _____.

- ◯ ripe
- ◯ role
- ◯ rate

7
We put them in a _____.

- ◯ bowl
- ◯ bait
- ◯ bite

8
Mom bakes a _____ with the berries.

- ◯ pay
- ◯ pie
- ◯ pole

Phonics, Second Grade SV 8862-5

Long Vowel u

Mule has the long **u** sound. The letters **u_e** can stand for the long **u** sound.

Write **u** and **e** under each picture that has the long **u** sound.

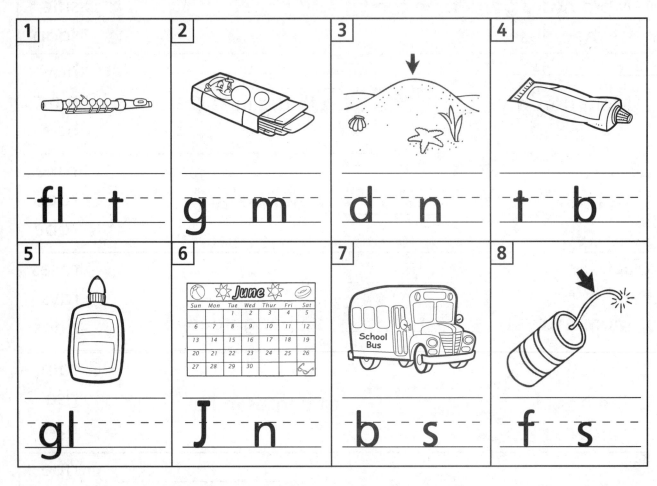

1	2	3	4
fl __ t	g __ __ m	d __ n	t __ b

5	6	7	8
gl __ __	J __ n	b __ s	f __ s

Write a sentence about the picture.

_____
- - - - - - - - - - - - - - - - - -
_____
- - - - - - - - - - - - - - - - - -
_____
- - - - - - - - - - - - - - - - - -
_____

Word Mix-up with Long Vowel u

Unscramble the letters to name each picture. Write the word on the line.

1		eubc	_____
2		utne	_____
3		lgeu	_____
4		betu	_____
5		seuf	_____
6		meul	_____
7		reupn	_____
8		tulfe	_____

Long Vowel e

Bee and **leaf** have the long **e** sound. The letters **ee** and **ea** can stand for the long **e** sound.

Circle the word that names each picture. Then write the word.
Circle the letters that stand for the long **e** sound.

1	eat eel east
2	peel peas please
3	feel feet feast
4	team tea tree
5	sleep sheep seem
6	seat sheet seal

Write a sentence about the picture.

Word Puzzle with Long Vowel e

Say the picture names. Write a word from the word box to name each picture. Then use the letters in the puzzle box to write an answer for the riddle.

bean	bee	heel	leaf	read	seat	weed

1. __ __ __ __

2. __ __ __ __

3. __ __ __ __

4. __ __ __ __

5. __ __ __ __

6. __ __ __ __

7. __ __ __ __

Riddle

What has one open eye but cannot see?

__ __   __ __ __ __

Maze with Long Vowels

Read each word. Color the box if the word has a long vowel sound. Then follow the path to find the home for the mice.

Start

toe	cube	hay	road
top	bag	sun	pie
bib	see	nail	team
bus	time	doll	net

Review Long Vowels

Darken the circle beside the word that completes each sentence. Then write the word on the line.

1

Not all plants _____ outside.

○ grow
○ goat
○ gave

2 You can grow some plants in your _____ _____, too.

○ hike
○ home
○ heat

3

Put the _____ in a pot filled with dirt.

○ seeds
○ sails
○ soaps

4

Your plants will _____ sun and water.

○ note
○ name
○ need

5

But don't _____ too much water.

○ oat
○ use
○ eat

6

Turn the pots every _____.

○ day
○ doe
○ die

7

Then each _____ will get light.

○ seem
○ same
○ side

8

You will have a _____ plant to look at.

○ fine
○ face
○ fuse

Vocabulary

Some words sound alike. But they have different spellings and different meanings.

> **sea** "the ocean"
> **see** "to look"
>
> **to** "in the direction of"
> **two** "the number after one"
>
> **its** "belonging to"
> **it's** "it is"

Write the word that correctly completes each sentence.

1 | _____

Mom and I went _____ visit Grandma.

to   two

2 | _____

Grandma lives by the _____.

sea   see

3 | _____

She likes to hear _____ gentle waves.

its   it's

4 | _____

We had not visited Grandma in _____ weeks.

to   two

5 | _____

I couldn't wait to _____ her.

sea   see

6 | _____

From our house, _____ a short drive.

its   it's

Squiggles

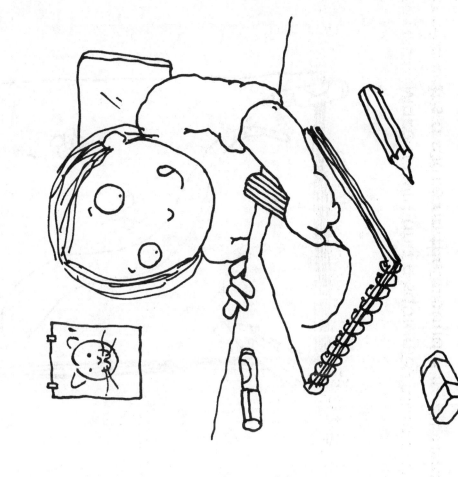

from a hen with a beak
to a fish floating in the sea!

Make a swirl and a squiggle.
It's a snake on the ground.

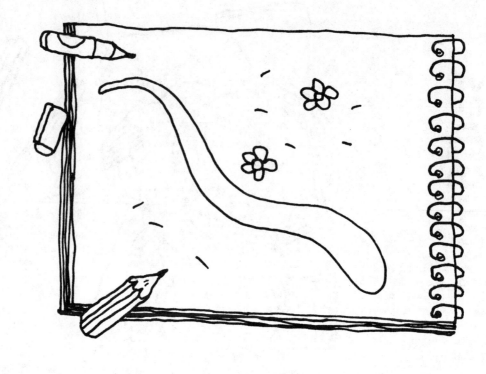

With a squiggle and some imagination,
you can make things like me—

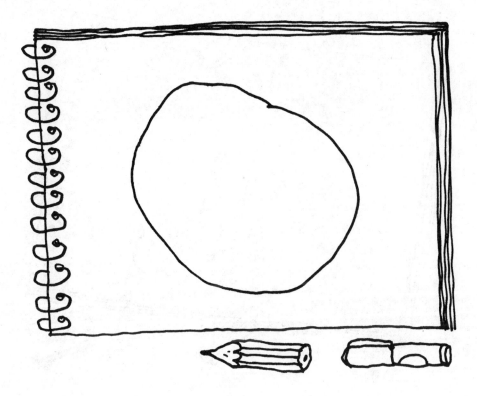

Make one more squiggle.
It's a stone, nice and round.

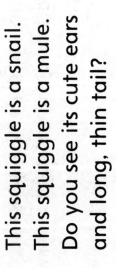

This squiggle is a snail.
This squiggle is a mule.
Do you see its cute ears
and long, thin tail?

This squiggle is a skunk
with stripes on its back.

This squiggle is a spider
with spots green and black.

Unit 4 Planner
Consonant Blends

Lesson	Phonemic Awareness	Phonics	Vocabulary	Comprehension and Fluency	Writing
Lesson 1 **Initial s Blends**	**Phoneme Identity:** *snake, snow, snap; skunk, skirt, skip* **Phoneme Segmentation:** *slip, spin, stamp*	Word Wheels with s Blends Activity Pages 78–79			Write tongue twisters with s blends.
Lesson 2 **Initial r Blends**	**Phoneme Identity:** *drum, dress, drop; grass, green, grapes* **Phoneme Segmentation:** *crib, frog, trunk*	Word Ladders with r Blends Activity Pages 80–81			Write riddles about things and actions whose names have r blends.
Lesson 3 **Initial l Blends**	**Phoneme Identity:** *flag, flat, fly; clock, clown, cloud* **Phoneme Segmentation:** *glad, sled, plant*	Word Building with l Blends Activity Pages 82–83			Write a paragraph about a clown that juggles things whose names have l blends.
Lesson 4 **Initial tw Blend**	**Phoneme Identity:** *twig, twenty, twirl* **Phoneme Segmentation:** *twin, twig, twist*	Word Wall with tw Activity Page 84 Review Initial Blends Activity Page 85			Write silly sentences with words that have the tw blend.
Lesson 5 **Final Blends**	**Phoneme Identity:** *jump, lamp, blimp; vest, wrist, fast* **Phoneme Segmentation:** *ant, belt, desk*	Crossword Puzzles with Final Blends Activity Pages 86–88 Review Final Blends Activity Page 89			Take a walk to find things in nature whose names have a final blend. Write the words in the Writer's Dictionary.
Lesson 6 **Story: "The Clouds"**			*crown, flash, fluffy, frown, scare, snuck, shapes, tower* Activity Page 90	Story Pages 91–94	

Unit 4: Consonant Blends

🦆 Develop Phonemic Awareness

You may wish to introduce the blends using these phonemic awareness techniques before students see the letter pairs.

• **Phoneme Identity** As you introduce each blend, say the corresponding groups of words below. Have children identify the two beginning sounds (or ending sounds) that all words have in common. Then challenge children to brainstorm other words that begin with the same blends. You may wish to explore other blends.

s blends:	(sn)	snake, snow, snap
	(sk)	skunk, skirt, skip
r blends:	(dr)	drum, dress, drop
	(gr)	grass, green, grapes
l blends:	(fl)	flag, flat, fly
	(cl)	clock, clown, cloud
tw blend:		twig, twenty, twirl
Final blends:	(mp)	jump, lamp, blimp
	(st)	vest, wrist, fast

• **Phoneme Segmentation** Tell children that you will sound out a word. Have them count the sounds they hear. Then have children repeat the phonemes and identify the word. Next, repeat the segmented word and help children write the word in their Writer's Dictionary. Suggest they circle the blend in each word.

s blends:	slip, spin, stamp
r blends:	crib, frog, trunk
l blends:	glad, sled, plant
tw blend:	twin, twig, twist
Final blends:	ant, belt, desk

🔤 Explore Phonics

Use these activities to help children explore consonant blends.

• **Word Wheels with s Blends** Invite children to make a word wheel using Master 1 on page 149. Ask them to write an s blend on the smaller wheel and phonograms on the larger wheel. Pair children and invite them to exchange the wheels and read the words.

• **Word Ladders with r Blends** Write each r blend on an index card. Tape each card along the base of a wall. Challenge children to write words they hear or read as well as draw pictures whose names begin with an r blend on index cards. Have them tape the cards to the appropriate "ladder."

• **Word Building with l Blends** Help children make a step book using Master 2 on page 150. Have them write a word with an l blend on the top page. On each tab, ask children to write instructions for changing one letter to form a new word. The new word is written above each instruction so it is hidden. For example, children write *clap* on the top page. The first tab will read "Change *a* to *i*." The word *clip* is hidden above the instructions on the tab. The second tab will read "Change *c* to *s*." The word *slip* is hidden above this instruction, and so on.

• **Word Wall with tw** Establish a word wall in which children contribute words they hear or read as well as pictures whose names begin with the tw blend.

• **Crossword Puzzles with Final Blends** Distribute Master 5 on page 153 to partners. Have children take turns writing words that end with final blends to form a crossword puzzle.

📖 Develop Vocabulary and Meaning

Blend Words

s blends:	scare, sky, slowly, smile, smiling, snuck, stop
r blends:	brown, crown, frown, Greg, ground, tree, trunk
l blends:	clouds, clown ('s), flash, floating, flowers, fluffy, playing, slowly
Final blends:	against, around, behind, cold, fast, ground, king, past, trunk

High-Frequency Words

a, and, another, but, by, can, comes, for, go, had, have, he, here, his, in, it, it's, likes, little, now, of, run, sees, that, the, then, they, to, was, what, with

Story Words

There are many story words. Review the story to choose words which children in your class will find most difficult.

Vocabulary Words

crown, flash, fluffy, frown, scare, snuck, shapes, tower

The following activities will help prepare children for reading the unit story independently. Afterwards, children can complete the vocabulary exercise on page 90.

• **Guess the Word** Introduce the vocabulary words by reading the clues below for children to guess the word. Write the words on the board as they are named.

It starts like top *and rhymes with* power.
  What word is it? (tower)

It starts like shop *and rhymes with* capes.
  What word is it? (shapes)

It starts like crab *and rhymes with* town.
  What word is it? (crown)

It starts like flute *and rhymes with* dash.
  What word is it? (flash)

It starts like friend *and rhymes with* down.
  What word is it? (frown)

It starts like snake *and rhymes with* duck.
  What word is it? (snuck)

It starts like fly *and rhymes with* stuffy.
  What word is it? (fluffy)

It starts like scale *and rhymes with* bear.
  What word is it? (scare)

• **Context Clues** Explain that an unknown word can be understood by looking at the words around it in a sentence. Write on the board, *We quietly snuck up close to the deer so that we would not scare it.* Model how the words *quietly* and *not scare* might give a clue to the meaning of *snuck*.

Read the Story: "The Clouds"

Before Reading

Display the cover of the book and read the title. Ask children to share experiences when they looked for shapes in clouds. Then invite children to page through the book to discover what cloud shapes the story character sees. Finally, ask children to follow along in their books as you read the story to see if their predictions are correct.

During Reading

• **Model Fluency** As you read the story aloud, model the fluency skills of reading poetry rhythmically, reading sentences with line breaks, and using appropriate expression for exclamatory sentences.

• **Model Comprehension** As you read the story aloud, you may wish to pause before words related to the cloud shapes and model how to decode the words using picture clues and sentence context.

After Reading

Have children find and read the words or phrases in the story that answer these questions:

What can Greg watch for hours? (clouds)

What did the king have on his head? (crown)

What did the bear do to the cat? (scare)

Do you think Greg will watch clouds again? Explain. (Answers will vary.)

Reread the Story: "The Clouds"

• **Choral Reading** Point out that the story is told in rhyme. Model reading the story, stressing the rhythm and rhyme. Then divide the class into two groups. One group will read the first two lines, and the second group will read the last two lines on each page.

• **Fluent Reading** Have partners turn to page 2. Point out that the first two lines are separate sentences but that the last two lines are one sentence. Model how to read a sentence of a poem when there are line breaks. Invite partners to take turns rehearsing the sentences on the page until they become fluid.

Connect the Story to Writing

• **Continue the Story** Invite children to suggest other things whose names begin or end with a blend that Greg might see in the clouds. Write each suggestion on the chalkboard using the sentence frame *Greg sees _____ in the clouds.* Then invite a volunteer to underline the letters that form the consonant blend in each word.

Support ESOL Learners

Children whose native language is Spanish may have problems with words that have *s* blends. Children whose native language is Chinese, Japanese, Korean, or Vietnamese may have problems with words that have *r* blends. Children whose native language is Chinese, Italian, Japanese, Korean, or Vietnamese may have problems with words that have *l* blends.

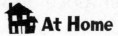

At Home

Encourage children to read "The Clouds" with someone at home. After reading, suggest they spend time outside looking at clouds and talking about the shapes they see.

s Blends

A **consonant blend** has two or more consonants that are next to each other. The sounds of the consonants blend together. But you can hear each sound. **Snake** begins with the consonant blend **sn**.

Look at the **s** blends in the box. Write the blend that you hear at the beginning of each picture name.

| sk | sl | sm | sn | sp | sq | st | sw |

| 1 | 2 | 3 | 4 |
| 5 | 6 | 7 | 8 |

Write a sentence about the picture.

_____

_____

_____

Name _____ Date _____

Word Games with s Blends

Say the picture names. Unscramble the letters to name each picture. Write the letters on the lines. Then use the letters in the circles to write an answer for the riddle.

1 lisan

2 semli

3 reots

4 snaw

5 krist

Riddle

What thing likes to have space?

___ ___ ___ ___ ___ ___

© Harcourt Achieve Inc.

Unit 4: Initial *s* Blends
Phonics, Second Grade SV 8862-5

Name _____   Date _____

r Blends

A **consonant blend** has two or more consonants that are next to each other. The sounds of the consonants blend together. But you can hear each sound. **Drum** begins with the consonant blend **dr**.

Look at the **r** blends in the box. Write the blend that you hear at the beginning of each picture name.

| br | cr | dr | fr | gr | pr | tr |

Write a sentence about the picture.

_____

_____

_____

_____

Word Games with r Blends

Change each word to name the picture. Add one letter to make a new word with an **r** blend.

1		bush
		_ _ _ _ _
2		rain
		_ _ _ _ _ _
3		room
		_ _ _ _ _
4		rip
		_ _ _ _ _
5		crow
		_ _ _ _
6		cane
		_ _ _ _ _

l Blends

A **consonant blend** has two or more consonants that are next to each other. The sounds of the consonants blend together. But you can hear each sound. **Flag** begins with the consonant blend **fl**.

Look at the **l** blends in the box. Write the blend that you hear at the beginning of each picture name.

bl	cl	fl	gl	pl	sl

| 1 | 2 | 3 | 4 |
| 5 | 6 | 7 | 8 |

Write a sentence about the picture.

_____

_____

_____

_____

www.svschoolsupply.com
© Harcourt Achieve Inc.

Unit 4: Initial l Blends
Phonics, Second Grade SV 8862-5

Rhyming Riddles with I Blends

Read each clue. Think about the word in dark print. Write a word that rhymes with that word and begins with an **I** blend to solve the riddle. The first one is done for you.

1 What kind of **block** tells time?

A <u>b</u> <u>l</u> <u>o</u> <u>c</u> <u>k</u>   <u>c</u> <u>l</u> <u>o</u> <u>c</u> <u>k</u>

2 What is a thin **hat**?

A __ __ __ __   <u>h</u> <u>a</u> <u>t</u>

3 What kind of **crow** does not fly fast?

A __ __ __ __   <u>c</u> <u>r</u> <u>o</u> <u>w</u>

4 What is a **red** toy that can slide down a snowy hill?

A <u>r</u> <u>e</u> <u>d</u>   __ __ __ __

5 What kind of **day** is filled with fun?

A __ __ __ __   <u>d</u> <u>a</u> <u>y</u>

6 What do you call a circus actor who falls **down**?

A <u>d</u> <u>o</u> <u>w</u> <u>n</u>   __ __ __ __

tw Blend

A **consonant blend** has two or more consonants that are next to each other. The sounds of the consonants blend together. But you can hear each sound. **Twig** begins with the consonant blend **tw**.

Write **tw** under each picture whose name begins like **twig**.

Write a sentence about the picture.

_____

- - - - - - - - - - - - - - - - - - -

_____

- - - - - - - - - - - - - - - - - - -

_____

Name _____ Date _____

Review Blends

Darken the circle beside the word that completes each sentence. Then write the word on the line.

1	The wind began to _____.	○ grow ○ blow ○ slow
2	The leaves on the _____ began to shake.	○ trees ○ please ○ freeze
3	The _____ began to block the sun.	○ clowns ○ clocks ○ clouds
4	Soon, the _____ turned black.	○ stars ○ sky ○ slip
5	It would begin to _____ any minute.	○ stop ○ storm ○ step
6	Small _____ of rain began to fall.	○ stops ○ flops ○ drops
7	They hit the dry _____.	○ ground ○ grade ○ grapes
8	People ran to find a safe _____ out of the rain.	○ plants ○ place ○ plane

Unit 4: Review Initial Blends
Phonics, Second Grade SV 8862-5

Name _____ Date _____

Final Blends

A **consonant blend** has two or more consonants that are next to each other. The sounds of the consonants blend together. But you can hear each sound. **Jump** ends with the consonant blend **mp**.

Look at the final blends in the box. Write the blend that you hear at the **end** of each picture name.

lt	mp	nd	nt	sk	st

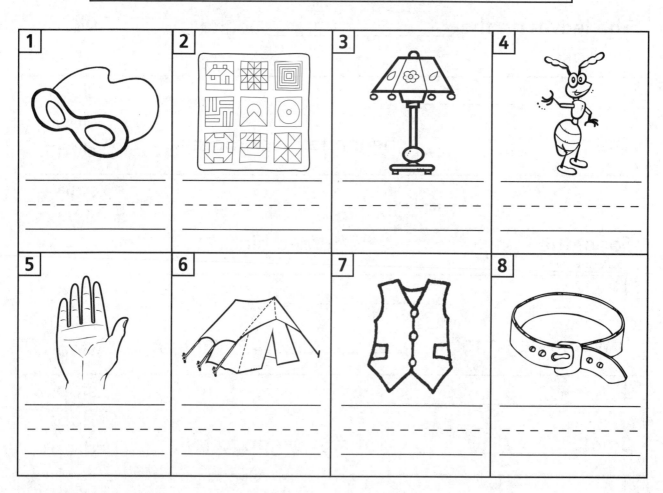

1	2	3	4

5	6	7	8

Write a sentence about the picture.

_____

_ _ _ _ _ _ _ _ _ _ _ _ _ _ _ _ _ _ _

_____

_ _ _ _ _ _ _ _ _ _ _ _ _ _ _ _ _ _ _

www.svschoolsupply.com
© Harcourt Achieve Inc.

Unit 4: Final Blends
Phonics, Second Grade SV 8862-5

Word Building with Final Blends

Follow the directions to build each word. Read each new word you write. Then circle the final blend in each word. Write the last word to answer the question.

---

1 What don't you want in your car? _____

Start with   **want**

a. Change **a** to **e** _____

b. Change **n** to **s** _____

c. Change **w** to **v** _____

d. Change **s** to **n** _____

e. Change **v** to **d** _____

---

2 Where do you keep a pet fish? _____

Start with   **desk**

a. Change **e** to **i** _____

b. Change **i** to **u** _____

c. Change **d** to **t** _____

d. Change **u** to **a** _____

e. Change **s** to **n** _____

---

3 What do you keep in a bank? _____

Start with   **hand**

a. Change **h** to **l** _____

b. Change **a** to **e** _____

c. Change **l** to **b** _____

d. Change **d** to **t** _____

e. Change **b** to **c** _____

Riddles with Final Blends

Write a word from th_____ _____wer each riddle.
Then circle the f_____

| ba_____ | | breakfast |
| desk_____ | stump | vest |

1. I am a place to keep money.
What am I?

_____

2. I am something you put on a
letter. What am I?

_____

3. I am a kind of meal.
What am I?

_____

4. I am a group of people who
play music. What am I?

_____

5. I am worn like a shirt, but I
don't have sleeves. What am I?

_____

6. I am something that is left when
a tree is cut down. What am I?

_____

7. I am something that holds up
your pants. What am I?

_____

8. I am a kind of furniture.
What am I?

_____

Name _____ Date _____

Review Final Blends

Darken the circle beside the word that completes each sentence. Then write the word on the line.

1 Dad and Ken looked for the perfect place

to _____ .

- ○ lump
- ○ limp
- ○ camp

2 Ken found a place by a _____

- ○ pond
- ○ kind
- ○ lend

3 "This is the _____ , ⌐ Dad.

- ○ best
- ○ gust
- ○ list

4 Soon Dad and Ken set up the _____ .

- ○ ant
- ○ dent
- ○ tent

5 Ken put a _____ inside so they could see at night.

- ○ ramp
- ○ lamp
- ○ damp

6 He put a warm _____ inside, too.

- ○ melt
- ○ quilt
- ○ tilt

7 Dad and Ken ate dinner at _____ .

- ○ mask
- ○ dusk
- ○ ask

8 Ken _____ very happy as he ate.

- ○ belt
- ○ built
- ○ felt

Vocabulary

Write a word from the box to complete
each sentence.

crown	flash	fluffy	frown
scare	snuck	shapes	tower

1. The cat was soft and _____.

2. We were very tired after climbing the stairs to the top

   of the _____.

3. The king wore a gold _____ on

   his head.

4. The children quietly _____ up

   behind their father to surprise him.

5. The people left the park when they saw a

   _____ of lightning.

6. The cook made cookies that had different

   _____.

7. Jen tried to _____ me when she

   yelled "BOO!"

8. Everyone knew that Greg was mad because he wore

   a _____ on his face.

The Clouds

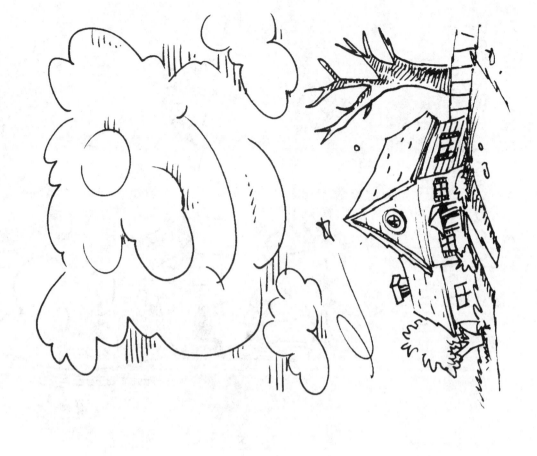

Run, Greg! It's time to go!
Here comes a cold, rainy shower.
You'll get to watch the clouds again,
Perhaps in another hour.

Greg sits on the ground by his house.
He leans against the trunk of a tree.
Greg likes to look up at the sky
To see what he can see.

The cow and the clown stop playing.
The clown's smile turns into a frown.
The clown bumps into the side of the cow,
And a flash of light comes down.

Greg watches the clouds for hours.
He sees shapes floating past.
Sometimes they move very slowly,
But sometimes they race really fast.

Now Greg sees a cow in the clouds,
Playing with a smiling clown.
But suddenly the sky changes quickly,
And the clouds turn a dark brown.

Today Greg saw a tall tower.
Then he saw a king with a crown.
The king had a big, fluffy cat
That was quietly running around.

Next, Greg saw two large flowers
And the head of a cute little bear.
The bear snuck up behind the cat
And gave it quite a scare.

Unit 5 Planner
Consonant Digraphs

Lesson	Phonemic Awareness	Phonics ABC	Vocabulary	Comprehension and Fluency	Writing
Lesson 1 **Initial Digraphs** *ch* and *wh*	**Phoneme Identity:** *chick, chair, cheese; wheel, whale, whisper* **Phoneme Segmentation:** *chop, whip, chest*	Word Wheel with Digraphs *ch* or *wh* Activity Pages 98–99			Write tongue twisters with digraphs *ch* and *wh*.
Lesson 2 **Initial Digraphs** *sh* and *th*	**Phoneme Identity:** *shoe, shell, sheep; thumb, thermos, third* **Phoneme Segmentation:** *ship, shade, think*	Word Wall with Digraphs *sh* and *th* Activity Pages 100–101			Write riddles about things and actions whose names have the digraphs *sh* or *th*.
Lesson 3 **Initial Digraphs** *kn* and *wr*	**Phoneme Identity:** *knight, knot, knock; wren, wreck, wring* **Phoneme Segmentation:** *wrap, knife, wrist*	Word Boxes with Digraphs *kn* and *wr* Activity Pages 102–103 Review Initial Digraphs Activity Page 104			Tell knock-knock jokes.
Lesson 4 **Final Digraphs**	**Phoneme Identity:** *(sh) fish, brush, cash; (nk) bank, think, hunk* **Phoneme Segmentation:** *path, catch, wing*	Word Dominoes with Final Digraphs Activity Pages 105–107 Review Final Digraphs Activity Pages 108–109			Take a walk around the school and playground to find things whose names have a final digraph. Write the words in the Writer's Dictionary.
Lesson 5 **Story: "Watch That Pitch!"**			*beautiful, catch, day, outside, play, sleeping* Activity Page 110	Story Pages 111–114	

Unit 5: Consonant Digraphs

Develop Phonemic Awareness

You may wish to introduce the digraphs using these phonemic awareness techniques before students see the letter pairs.

• **Phoneme Identity** As you introduce each digraph, say the corresponding groups of words below. Have children identify the beginning sound (or ending sound for final digraphs) that all words have in common. Then challenge children to brainstorm other words that have the same sound.

  ch and *wh*: chick, chair, cheese
       wheel, whale, whisper
  sh and *th*: shoe, shell, sheep
       thumb, thermos, third
  kn and *wr*: knight, knot, knock
       wren, wreck, wring
 Final Digraphs: (*sh*) fish, brush, cash
       (*nk*) bank, think, hunk

• **Phoneme Segmentation** Tell children that you will sound out a word. Have them count the sounds they hear. Then have children repeat the phonemes and identify the word. Next, repeat the segmented word and help children write the word in their Writer's Dictionary. Suggest they circle the digraph in each word.

  ch and *wh*: chop, whip, chest
  sh and *th*: ship, shade, think
  kn and *wr*: wrap, knife, wrist
 Final Digraphs: path, catch, wing

Explore Phonics

Use these activities to help children explore consonant digraphs.

• **Word Wheel with Digraphs *ch* or *wh***
Invite children to make a word wheel using Master 1 on page 149. Ask them to write a *ch* or *wh* digraph on the smaller wheel and phonograms on the larger wheel. Pair children and invite them to exchange the wheels and read the words.

• **Word Wall with Digraphs *sh* and *th***
Establish a word wall in which children contribute words they hear or read that have the digraphs *sh* and *th*. Have children write words with *sh* on red rectangles and words with *th* on blue rectangles.

• **Word Boxes with Digraphs *kn* and *wr***
Using the grid from Master 4 on page 152, write 16 words that that have *kn* or *wr*. Copy the page and pair children. To play the game, players each choose a crayon. Have partners take turns reading a word and coloring the square if the word is read correctly. The player coloring the most squares wins.

• **Word Dominoes with Final Digraphs**
Using the grid from Master 4 on page 152, cut the boxes apart so that two boxes remain joined. Write 16 words that end with a digraph on eight of the "dominoes." Repeat with the other dominoes. Partners play the game by matching words and reading them aloud.

Develop Vocabulary and Meaning

Digraph Words

    ch: chair, chase, children, chin
    sh: shining, should
    th: that, the, there, things
   wh: what, when, whistled
Final Digraphs: catch, each, lunch, Mitch,
        ouch, pitch, search, song, watch

High-Frequency Words

a, could, for, he, his, it, many, not, on, that, the, to, too, was, we, were

Story Words

There are many story words. Review the story to choose the words which children in your class will find most difficult.

Vocabulary Words

beautiful, catch, day, outside, play, sleeping

The following activities will help prepare children for reading the unit story independently. Afterwards, children can complete the vocabulary exercise on page 110.

• **Synonyms** Write the following words on index cards: *beautiful, chase, hit, pitch, play, search, shining, song, wanted, watch*. Lay the cards face up on a table. Say word clues that are synonyms of the written words. Volunteers find the matching card and read the word aloud.

• **Word Baseball** Write digraph, vocabulary, and story words on index cards. Divide the children into two teams. Identify four places to be the bases in a baseball field. Play baseball by giving children cards to read. Words that are read incorrectly count as an out. Children advance one base as each card is read correctly. Runs are scored when a child visits all the bases.

• **Antonyms** Explain that some words can have opposite meanings. Challenge children to act out antonyms for different words: *open (close), happy (sad), up (down), sleep (awake)*.

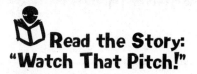

Read the Story: "Watch That Pitch!"

Before Reading

Display the cover of the book and read the title. Discuss the meaning of the word *pitch*. Have children speculate what the story might be about. Then ask children to follow along in their books as you read the story to see if their predictions are correct.

During Reading

• **Model Fluency** As you read the story aloud, model the fluency skills of reading words in quotation marks, reading sentences with line breaks, and using appropriate expression for questions.

• **Model Comprehension** You may wish to model how to identify the main idea by asking: *What is this story mostly about?*

After Reading

Have children find and read the words or phrases in the story that answer these questions:

Who are the characters in the story? (Mitch and his friends)

What did the children play? (catch)

What did the bird do? (whistle a song)

Why will Mitch watch pitches now? (He does not want to be hit by the ball again.)

Reread the Story: "Watch That Pitch!"

• **Act It Out** Invite two children to play the roles of Mitch and the pitcher and act out the story while you or members of the group read the story aloud.

• **Retell the Story** Have children retell the story as Mitch might tell it. Encourage them to describe, from Mitch's own point of view, the day and the things that caught his attention and kept him from watching the ball.

• **Fluent Reading** Have partners turn to page 2. Explain that quotation marks signal that a character in the story is speaking. Model how the character might read the question. Invite partners to take turns rehearsing the quotation as if they were Mitch.

Connect the Story to Writing

• **Make a List** Explain that Mitch found out that it was very important to watch each pitch to stay safe. Challenge children to write a list of other things that Mitch should do to play ball safely.

🌐 Support ESOL Learners

Students whose native language is Chinese, French, Greek, Japanese, or Spanish may have problems with *ch* and *wh* words. Students whose native language is Chinese, French, Italian, Japanese, Korean, Urdu, or Vietnamese may have problems with *sh* and *th* words.

🏠 At Home

Encourage children to read "Watch That Pitch!" with someone at home. After reading, suggest they spend time playing catch.

Digraphs ch and wh

chair   whale

A **consonant digraph** has two consonants that are next to each other. They stand for one sound.

Write **ch** or **wh** to show the beginning sound in each picture name.

| 1 | 2 | 3 | 4 |
| 5 | 6 | | |

Write a sentence about the picture.

_____
- - - - - - - - - - - - - - - - - -
_____
- - - - - - - - - - - - - - - - - -
_____

Word Games with Digraphs ch and wh

Say the picture names. Unscramble the letters to name each picture. Write the letters on the lines. Then use the letters in circles to write an answer for the riddle.

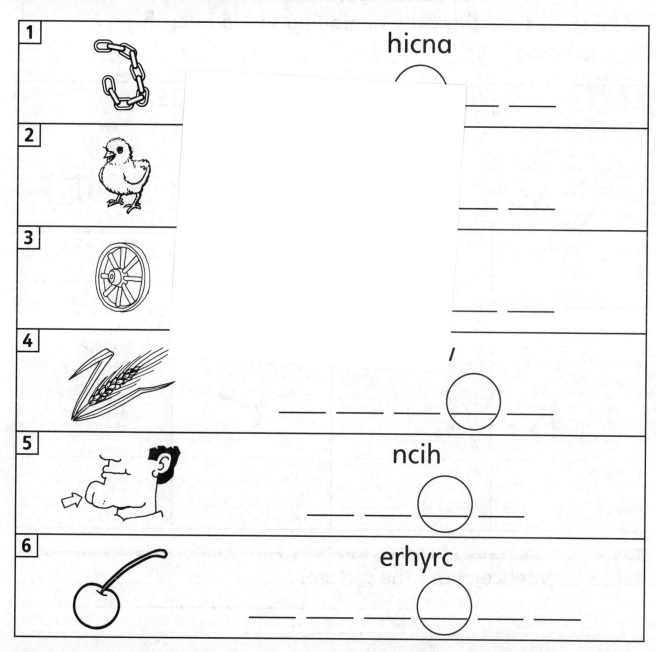

1 hicna

2

3

4

5 ncih

6 erhyrc

Riddle

What has arms and legs but no face?

___ ___   ___ ___ ___ ___

Digraphs sh and th

shoe   thumb

A **consonant digraph** has two consonants that are next to each other. They stand for one sound.

Write **sh** or **th** to show the beginning sound in each picture name.

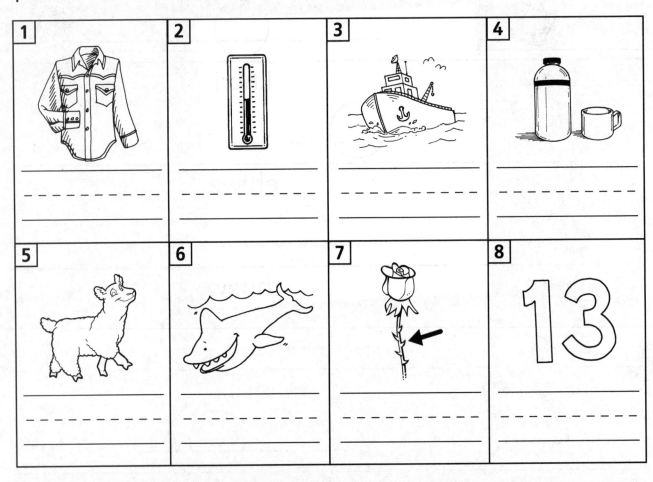

Write a sentence about the picture.

_____
_____
_____
_____
_____

Crossword Puzzle with Digraphs **sh** and **th**

Read each clue. Write a word from the box to complete the puzzle.

shark	shell
shirt	shovel
think	thorn
thumb	

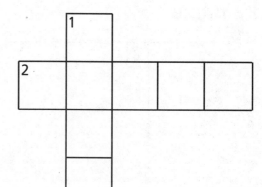

Across

2. A part of the hand
4. An ocean animal
6. The outer part of an egg
7. Something people wear

Down

1. To use the mind to make ideas
3. Something to dig with
5. Something sharp on the stem of a rose

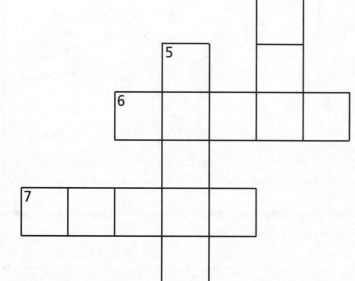

Digraphs kn and wr

knight   **write**

A **consonant digraph** has two consonants that are next to each other. They stand for one sound.

Write **kn** or **wr** to show the beginning sound in each picture name.

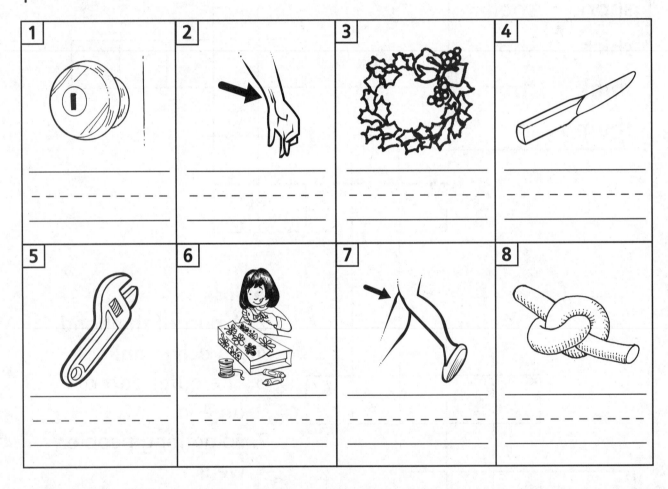

1

2

3

4

5

6

7

8

___

Write a sentence about the picture.

_____

Word Find for Digraphs **kn** and **wr**

Read the words in the box. Find each word in the puzzle and circle it. The words go across and down.

knee	knit	knock	know
wreck	wring	write	wrong

a	b	f	d	g	h	w	p
r	e	k	n	o	w	r	e
w	r	e	c	k	r	i	k
c	d	h	e	t	f	t	n
k	n	i	t	j	b	e	o
n	u	f	l	r	t	p	c
e	n	w	r	i	n	g	k
e	y	h	p	b	t	g	u
z	b	w	r	o	n	g	s

Name _____ Date _____

Review Digraphs

Darken the circle beside the word that completes each sentence. Then write the word on the line.

1

Mr. Ruiz took a ride on a _____.

○ ship
○ whip
○ chip

2

He saw a _____ swimming in the water.

○ shade
○ whale
○ chair

3

Mr. Ruiz also saw a _____ with sharp teeth.

○ chart
○ shark
○ wrap

4

It began to _____ a school of fish.

○ thank
○ what
○ chase

5

Mr. Ruiz walked on the sand _____ the ship stopped.

○ when
○ then
○ wren

6

He found _____ shells.

○ shirt
○ chirp
○ thirty

7

Mr. Ruiz will use them to make

a _____ to hang on the door.

○ wreath
○ cheese
○ sheet

8

People who _____ on the door will see it.

○ shop
○ knock
○ chop

Final Digraphs ch and wh

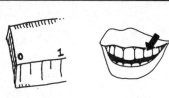

inch   tooth

A **consonant digraph** has two consonants that are next to each other. They stand for one sound. Consonant digraphs can be at the end of words.

Write **ch** or **th** to show the ending sound in each picture name.

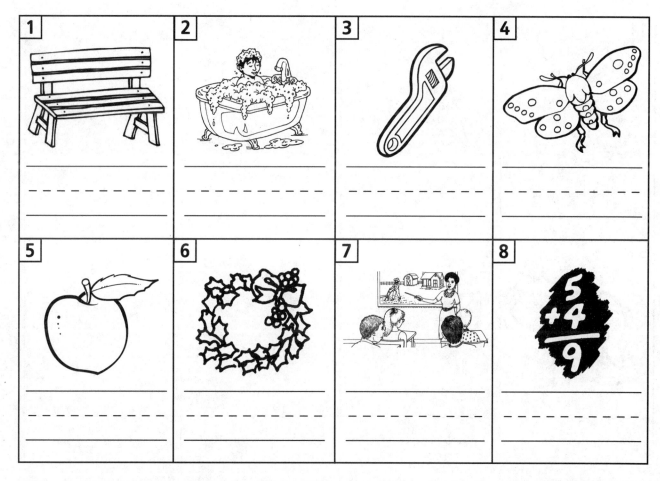

1	2	3	4
_ _ _ _ _	_ _ _ _ _	_ _ _ _ _	_ _ _ _ _
5	6	7	8
_ _ _ _ _	_ _ _ _ _	_ _ _ _ _	_ _ _ _ _

Write a sentence about the picture.

_____

_ _ _ _ _ _ _ _ _ _ _ _ _ _ _

_____

_ _ _ _ _ _ _ _ _ _ _ _ _ _ _

_____

Final Digraphs **ng** and **nk**

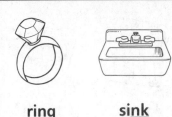

ring   **si**_nk_

A **consonant digraph** has two consonants that are next to each other. They stand for one sound. Consonant digraphs can be at the end of words.

Write **ng** or **nk** to show the ending sound in each picture name.

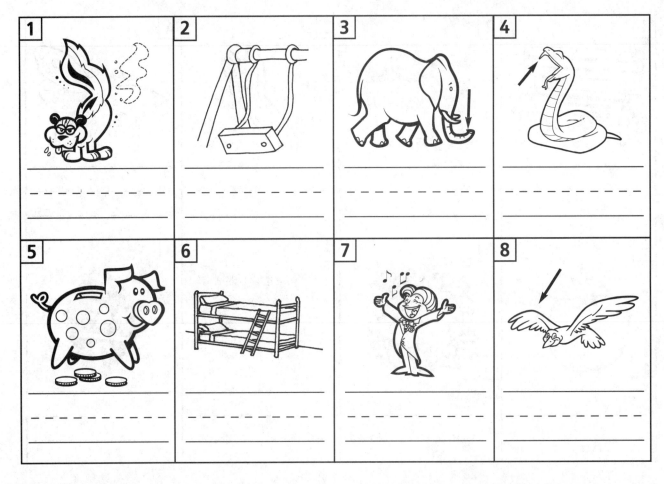

Write a sentence about the picture.

_____
_____
_____
_____

Final Digraphs ck, sh, and tch

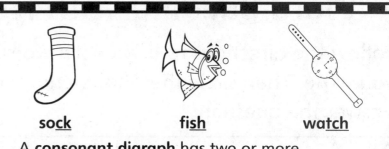

sock **fish** **watch**

A **consonant digraph** has two or more consonants that are next to each other. They stand for one sound. Consonant digraphs can be at the end of words.

Write **ck, sh,** or **tch** to show the ending sound in each picture name.

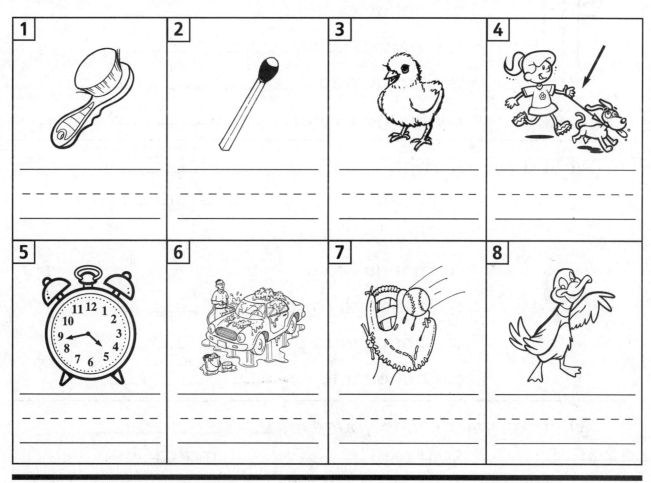

Write a sentence about the picture.

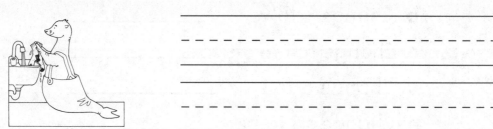

Word Building with Final Digraphs

Follow the directions to build each word. Read each new word you write. Then circle the final blend. Write the last word to answer the question.

1 What can you do with a bell? _____

Start with   __knock__

a. Change **kn** to **s**   _____

b. Change **ck** to **ng**   _____

c. Change **s** to **wr**   _____

d. Change **o** to **i**   _____

e. Change **wr** to **r**   _____

2 What do you do with a ball? _____

Start with   __fish__

a. Change **f** to **w**   _____

b. Change **i** to **a**   _____

c. Change **sh** to **tch**   _____

d. Change **w** to **p**   _____

e. Change **a** to **i**   _____

3 What can you do with your eye? _____

Start with   __match__

a. Change **m** to **c**   _____

b. Change **c** to **w**   _____

c. Change **tch** to **sh**   _____

d. Change **a** to **i**   _____

e. Change **sh** to **nk**   _____

Review Final Digraphs

Darken the circle beside the word that completes each sentence. Then write the word on the line.

1
_____
The _____ run to the lake.
- ○ shells
- ○ wheels
- ○ children

2
_____
They look at the _____ swimming in the water.
- ○ teeth
- ○ fish
- ○ fifth

3
_____
Soon they take off their _____.
- ○ shoes
- ○ cheese
- ○ knights

4
_____
They swim and _____ in the water.
- ○ splash
- ○ thumb
- ○ wrist

5
_____
Ken bumps his _____ on a rock.
- ○ sock
- ○ knee
- ○ whale

6
_____
"_____!" Ken cries.
- ○ Ring
- ○ Chin
- ○ Ouch

7 Ken gets out and begins to dig with a
_____.
- ○ shovel
- ○ chick
- ○ thin

8
_____
He _____ a tune as he digs.
- ○ watches
- ○ wishes
- ○ whistles

Vocabulary

Draw lines to match the pictures that have opposite meanings. Then use words from the box to write the name of the pictures in the last column.

beautiful	catch	day	outside	play	sleeping

1.

night

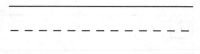

2.

inside

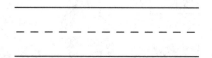

3.

ugly

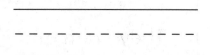

4.

work

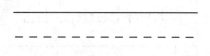

5.

throw

6.

waking

Watch That Pitch!

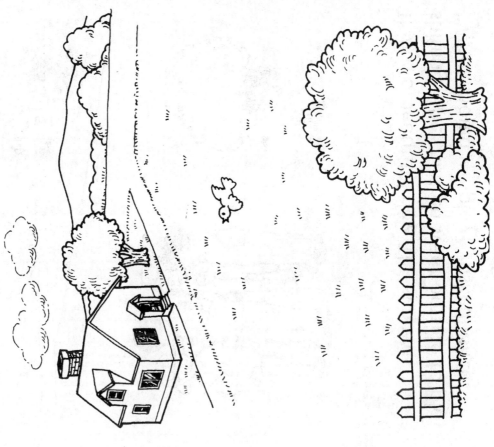

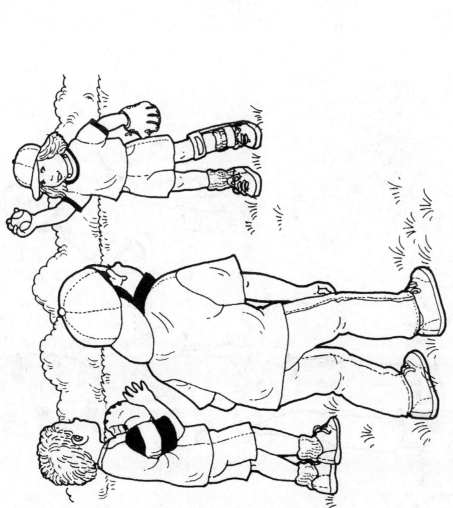

After that, Mitch watched each pitch
when he played catch.

It was a beautiful day. The sun was
shining. The children went outside to play.
"What should we play?" asked Mitch.

Ouch! The ball hit Mitch on the chin.

The children decided to play catch.
Soon it was Mitch's turn to catch
the ball.

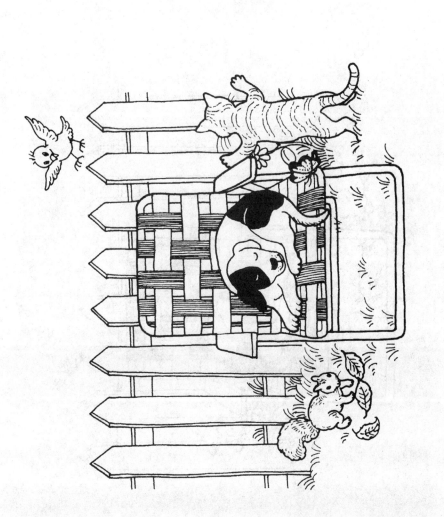

Mitch could watch the cat chase the bird.
He could watch the squirrel search
for lunch.

Mitch could not keep his eye on the ball. There were too many things that he wanted to watch.

He could watch the bird as it whistled a song. He could watch the dog sleeping in the chair.

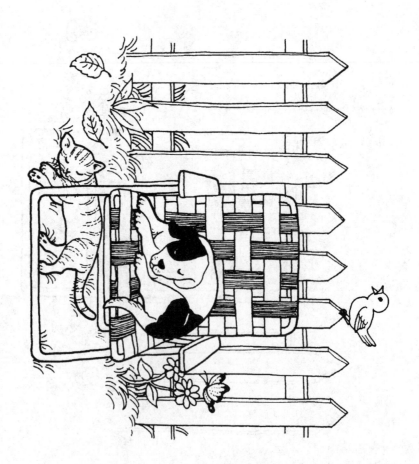

Unit 6 Planner
r-Controlled Vowels and y as a Vowel

Lesson	Phonemic Awareness	Phonics ABC	Vocabulary	Comprehension and Fluency	Writing
Lesson 1 **Vowels *ar* and *or***	**Phoneme Identity:** *car, farm, yard; corn, fork, horse* **Phoneme Segmentation:** *jar, horn, storm*	Word Ladders with Vowels *ar* and *or* Activity Page 118			Write rhyming couplets using words that have the vowel sounds of *ar* or *or*.
Lesson 2 **Vowels *er, ir,* and *ur***	**Phoneme Identity:** *herd, girl, nurse* **Phoneme Segmentation:** *fern, first, fur*	Word Wall with Vowels *er, ir,* and *ur* Activity Page 119 Review *r*-Controlled Vowels Activity Pages 120–121			Write a paragraph about the job of a nurse. Use words that have the /ur/ sound.
Lesson 3 **y as a Vowel**	**Phoneme Identity:** *cry, fly, spy; baby, city, happy* **Phoneme Segmentation:** *my, lady, candy*	Word Sort with *y* as a Vowel Activity Page 122 Review *y* as a Vowel Activity Page 123			Write a sentence using words that have the long *i* and long *e* sounds for *y*.
Lesson 4 **Story: "Before the Storm"**			*chores, clouds, farmer, hurry, sky, socks* Activity Page 124	Story Pages 125–128	

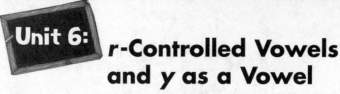

Develop Phonemic Awareness

You may wish to introduce the vowels using these phonemic awareness techniques before students see the spelling patterns.

• **Phoneme Identity** As you introduce each vowel, say the corresponding groups of words below. Have children identify the sound that all words have in common. Then challenge children to brainstorm other words that have the same sound.

ar and *or*:	car, farm, yard
	corn, fork, horse
er, ir, and *ur*:	herd, girl, nurse
y as a vowel:	cry, fly, spy
	baby, city, happy

• **Phoneme Segmentation** Tell children that you will sound out a word. Have them count the sounds they hear. Then have children repeat the phonemes and identify the word. Next, repeat the segmented word and help children write the word in their Writer's Dictionary. Suggest they circle the letters that stand for the vowel sound in each word. You may wish to discuss the challenges children can face when trying to spell words that have the *er, ir,* or *ur* spelling patterns.

ar and *or*:	jar, horn, storm
er, ir, and *ur*:	fern, first, fur
y as a vowel:	my, lady, candy

Explore Phonics

Use these activities to help children explore *r*-controlled vowels and *y* as a vowel.

• **Word Ladders with Vowels *ar* and *or***
Write words that have the *r*-controlled vowels *ar* and *or*, including *car* and *corn*, on index cards. Tape the cards with *car* and *corn* along the bottom of a wall. Then pass out the remaining cards to children. Help each child read the word and tape the card above the word with the matching vowel sound to form a "ladder."

• **Word Wall with Vowels *er, ir,* and *ur***
Establish a word wall in which children contribute words they hear or read that have the *r*-controlled vowels *er, ir,* and *ur*. Have children write words with *er* on red rectangles, words with *ir* on blue rectangles, and words with *ur* on yellow rectangles.

• **Word Sort with *y* as a Vowel** Using the grid from Master 4 on page 152, write 16 words that have *y* as a vowel. Invite children to cut the boxes apart and sort them into groups with the long *e* and long *i* sounds.

Develop Vocabulary and Meaning

r-Controlled Vowel and *y* as a Vowel Words

ar: barn, dark, darker, far, farm, farmer, start, started

or: before, chore, chores, corn, fork, form, horse, store, storm

er: another, farmer, her, herself

ir: first, shirt, third

ur: hurry, turned

y: dry, happy, hurry, sky

High-Frequency Words

a, and, another, at, but, do, got, had, her, in, it, not, now, on, put, she, that, the, then, there, they, to, too, up, was, with, would

Story Words

away, began, didn't, hay, looked, mind, second, soon, stay, them, yes

Vocabulary Words

chores, clouds, farmer, hurry, sky, socks

The following activities will help prepare children for reading the unit story independently. Afterwards, children can complete the vocabulary exercise on page 124.

• **Storm Mobiles** In advance, cut out cloud shapes from gray paper and raindrop shapes from light blue paper. Then cut yarn into various lengths. In class, assign partners an *r*-controlled vowel or the vowel *y*. Have each pair write their vowel on a cloud. Then have them search "Before the Storm" for words in the text that have the assigned vowel spelling. Ask children to write each word on a raindrop. Next, invite them to attach the drops to the cloud by stapling the pieces to yarn. Invite partners to share their storm mobiles by reading aloud the words.

• **Dictionary Skills** Have children page through a dictionary. Remind them that a dictionary tells how to spell a word and gives its meaning. Direct children to look at the pronunciation key. Then practice using the pronunciation key to read the words *can* and *cane*. Help children look for them in the dictionary. Help children explore the pronunciations and the definitions.

Read the Story: "Before the Storm"

Before Reading

Display the cover of the book and read the title. Lead children in a discussion of where the story takes place and what might happen in the story. Then ask children to follow along in their books as you read the story to see if their observations are correct.

During Reading

• **Model Fluency** As you read the story aloud, model the fluency skills of reading sentences with line breaks and using appropriate expression for questions and exclamations.

• **Model Comprehension** You may wish to model how to identify the story plot by drawing a simple flow chart and helping children list the sequence of events as they read along. Point out how the use of time-order words helps the reader to understand the order of the actions.

After Reading

Have children find and read the words or phrases in the story that answer these questions:

Where does the story take place? (on a farm)

What does the farmer do first? (get the corn)

Why does the farmer go into the barn? (to stay dry)

Why is it unsafe to stay outside in a storm? (Answers will vary.)

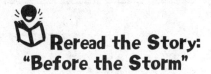

Reread the Story: "Before the Storm"

• **Retell the Story** Invite children to pretend they are the farmer and to tell about the events in the story as if they were telling it to some friends the next day.

• **Fluent Reading** Have partners turn to page 7. Explain that a question mark signals that the voice should rise at the end of a sentence. Model how to read the question with the voice unchanging and then with the voice rising. Discuss the difference. Then invite partners to take turns reading the question to practice fluency.

 Connect the Story to Writing

• **Innovate on the Story** Challenge children to choose a new setting and character to create their own version of "Before the Storm." Have them tell what the new character must do before the storm arrives.

 Support ESOL Learners

Children may be confused by the use of *-er* as a suffix. Write the skill words *farmer* and *darker* on the chalkboard. Explain that when *-er* is added to a word that names a place or activity, it makes a word that names a person who does something. For example, a farmer works on a farm. But when *-er* is added to a word that describes, like *dark*, it makes the word mean "more." *Darker* means "more dark."

 **At Home**

Encourage children to read "Before the Storm" with someone at home. Suggest that after reading they talk about storms— how to tell when a storm is coming and precautions to take if a person is outside when the storm arrives.

Vowels **ar** and **or**

car   corn

When **r** follows a vowel, it changes the vowel sound.

Say each picture name. Write **ar** if you hear the same vowel sound in **car**. Write **or** if you hear the same vowel sound in **corn**.

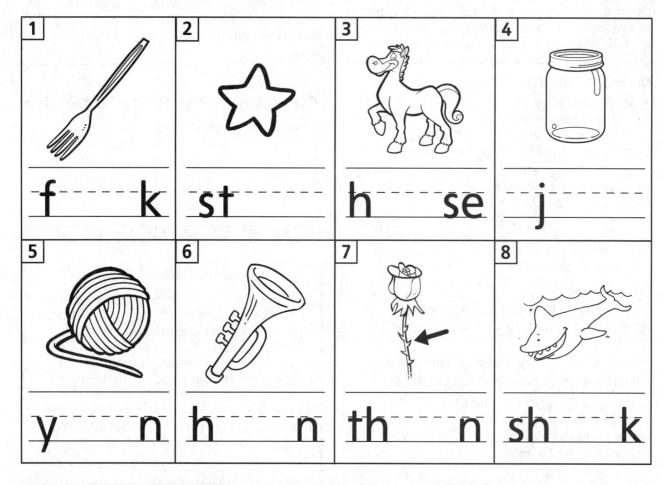

1. f___k
2. st___
3. h___se
4. j___
5. y___n
6. h___n
7. th___n
8. sh___k

Write a sentence about the picture.

_____
_____
_____
_____

Vowels er, ir, and ur

fern   bird   nurse

When **r** follows a vowel, it changes the vowel sound. The letter pairs **er**, **ir**, and **ur** all have the same sound.

Circle the word that names each picture. Then write the word.

1
person
purse
perk
_____

2
stir
skirt
shirt
_____

3
hurl
herd
hurt
_____

4
germ
girl
gerbil
_____

5
churn
chirp
church
_____

6
surf
sir
spur
_____

Write a sentence about the picture.

_____
_____
_____
_____
_____

Phonics, Second Grade SV 8862-5

Group Words with r-Controlled Vowels

Circle the words that belong.

1

Which are places?

barn	burn	church	park	pork
fort	form	yard	yarn	born

2

Which are animals?

stork	start	short	shark	horse
horn	bird	lark	sharp	shirt

3

Which can you hear?

horn	snarl	harm	organ	harp
chirp	part	purr	smart	snort

4

Which are on a farm?

born	barn	horse	star	corn
word	dirt	hard	dark	herd

5

Which can you wear?

sport	spur	shorts	storm	scarf
star	stern	shirt	fork	skirt

Name _____ Date _____

Review r-Controlled Vowels

Darken the circle beside the word that completes each sentence. Then write the word on the line.

1

_____

Mort lives on a _____.

○ fern
○ farm
○ far

2

_____

He grows _____.

○ churn
○ curls
○ corn

3

_____

Mort has cows and _____.

○ hurts
○ horns
○ horses

4

_____

They need a clean _____.

○ born
○ barn
○ burst

5

_____

Mort plants seeds in the _____.

○ dirt
○ darn
○ dart

6

_____

The _____ like to eat the seeds.

○ burns
○ barks
○ birds

7

_____

Mort loads up his _____.

○ cart
○ cord
○ curl

8 At the end of the day, Mort sits on his

_____.

○ part
○ porch
○ perk

y as a Vowel

fl**y**   pupp**y**

The letter **y** has two sounds. It can have the long **i** sound that you hear in **fly**. It can have the long **e** sound that you hear in **puppy**.

Circle the word that names each picture. Then write the word. Circle the pictures whose names have the **long e** sound like **puppy**.

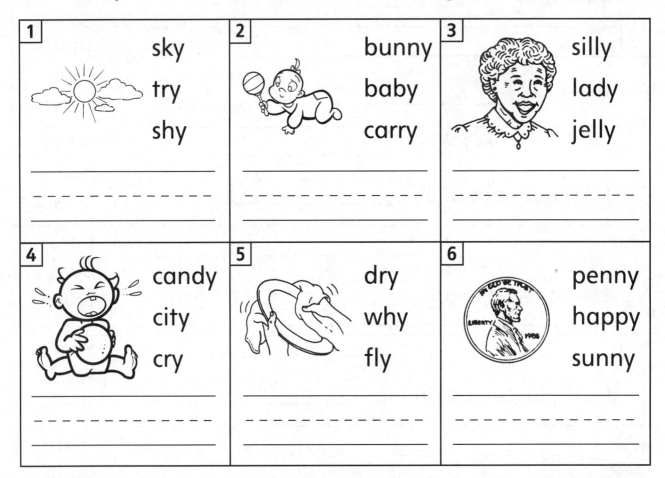

1   sky   try   shy

2   bunny   baby   carry

3   silly   lady   jelly

4   candy   city   cry

5   dry   why   fly

6   penny   happy   sunny

Write a sentence about the picture.

_____
_____
_____
_____
_____

Review y as a Vowel

Darken the circle beside the word that completes each sentence.
Then write the word on the line.

1 What kind of pet would make you

_____
- - - - - - - - - - - -
_____ ?

○ hay
○ happy
○ handy

2
_____
- - - - - - - - - -
My pal Penny has _____ little fish.

○ try
○ tray
○ twenty

3
_____
- - - - - - - - - -
Maybe you would like a soft _____ .

○ bunny
○ boy
○ by

4
_____
- - - - - - - - - -
A little _____ would be fun, too.

○ pay
○ puppy
○ penny

5
_____
- - - - - - - - - -
Would you rather have a _____
kitten?

○ tiny
○ fly
○ city

6
_____
- - - - - - - - - -
_____ animals need extra care.

○ Bay
○ Baby
○ Body

7
_____
- - - - - - - - - -
Some animals _____ all the time.

○ cry
○ clay
○ copy

8
_____
- - - - - - - - - -
Others are very quiet and _____ .

○ sky
○ story
○ shy

Vocabulary

Look at the way a dictionary tells how to sound out words.
Write a word from the word box that shows how the word looks
in the dictionary. Then draw a line to the matching picture.

a	add	e	end	o	odd	o͞o	pool	oi	oil	t͟h	this
ā	ace	ē	equal	ō	open	u	up	ou	pout	zh	vision
â	care	i	it	ô	order	û	burn	ng	ring		
ä	car	ī	ice	o͝o	took	yo͞o	fuse	th	thin		

ə = { a in *above*   e in *sicken*   i in *possible*
      o in *melon*   u in *circus* }

chores	clouds	farmer	hurry	sky	socks

1. /färm´ ûr/ _ _ _ _ _ _ _ _ _ _ _ _

2. /soks/ _ _ _ _ _ _ _ _ _ _ _ _ _

3. /chôrz/ _ _ _ _ _ _ _ _ _ _ _ _

4. /hûr´ ē/ _ _ _ _ _ _ _ _ _ _ _ _

5. /klowdz/ _ _ _ _ _ _ _ _ _ _ _ _

6. /skī/ _ _ _ _ _ _ _ _ _ _ _ _ _

Before the Storm

Yes! The farmer put herself in the barn. And then it started to storm. But the farmer didn't mind. She was happy and dry.

A farmer looked up at the sky.
Dark clouds began to form. A storm
would start soon.

Third, the farmer got her shirt and socks.
She would store them in the barn, too.
Was there another chore that the farmer
had to do before the storm?

The sky turned darker and darker.
The farmer had to hurry. The storm
was not far away.

Second, the farmer got the horse.
She put it in the barn. Now the horse
would stay dry.

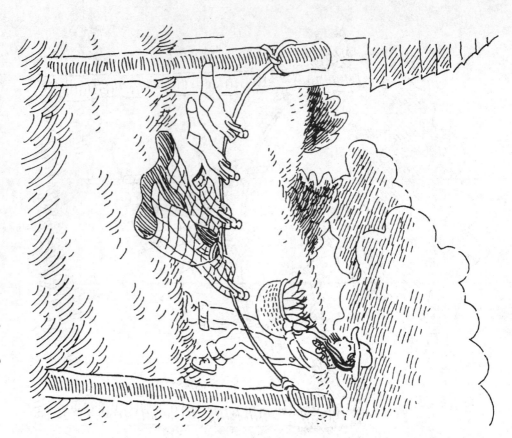

Before it started to storm, the farmer had to do chores on the farm. First, she got the corn.

The farmer put the corn in the barn with the hay fork. They would stay dry.

Unit 7 Planner
Vowel Digraphs and Diphthongs

Lesson	Phonemic Awareness	Phonics	Vocabulary	Comprehension and Fluency	Writing
Lesson 1 **Vowel Digraphs** *ea* and *oo*	**Phoneme Identity:** *tea, bead, meat; head, bread, sweat; book, wool, hood; zoo, moon, stool* **Phoneme Blending:** *tea, bread, book, moon*	Word Ladders with Digraphs *ea* and *oo* Activity Pages 132–133 Review *ea* and *oo* Activity Page 134			Write a paragraph about a day spent at the beach. Include words that have the vowel digraphs *ea* and *oo*.
Lesson 2 **Vowel Digraphs** *ue, ui, ew, au, aw,* and *al*	**Phoneme Identity:** *blue, fruit, screw; haul, paw, ball* **Phoneme Blending:** *glue, suit, new; fault, lawn, salt*	Word Walls with Digraphs *ue, ui, ew* and *au, aw, al* Activity Pages 135–136 Review *ue, ui, ew* and *au, aw, al* Activity Page 137 Review Digraphs Activity Page 138			Write riddles about things and actions whose names have the vowel digraphs *ue, ui, ew, au, aw,* and *al*.
Lesson 3 **Vowel Diphthongs** *oi, oy, ow,* and *ou*	**Phoneme Identity:** *boy, coins, oil; cow, town, brown; mow, bowl, snow; mouse, brown, cloud* **Phoneme Blending:** *toy, point; crow, town; out, crown*	Word Ladders with Vowel Diphthongs Activity Pages 139–141 Review Vowel Diphthongs Activity Pages 142–143			List things that can be found on a farm. Circle the words that have vowel diphthongs.
Lesson 4 **Story: "Sue Had the Flu"**			*close, enjoy, laugh, quick, right, sick, stare, well* Activity Page 144	Story Pages 145–148	

🗣 Develop Phonemic Awareness

You may wish to introduce the vowel digraphs and diphthongs using these phonemic awareness techniques before students see the spelling patterns.

• **Phoneme Identity** As you introduce each digraph or dipthong, say the corresponding groups of words below. Have children identify the sound that all words have in common. Then challenge children to brainstorm other words that have the same sound.

ea:	tea, bead, meat head, bread, sweat
oo:	book, wool, hood zoo, moon, stool
ue, ui, and *ew:*	blue, fruit, screw
au, aw, and *al:*	haul, paw, ball
oi and *oy:*	boy, coins, oil
ow:	cow, town, brown mow, bowl, snow
ow and *ou:*	mouse, brown, cloud

• **Phoneme Blending** Tell children that you will sound out a word. Have them count the sounds they hear. Then have children repeat the phonemes and blend the word. Write the word on the chalkboard. You may wish to have children include the word in their Writer's Dictionary. Discuss the challenges children can face when trying to spell words that have vowel digraphs and diphthongs.

ea:	tea, bread
oo:	book, moon
ue, ui, and *ew:*	glue, suit, new
au, aw, and *al:*	fault, lawn, salt
oi and *oy:*	toy, point
ow:	crow, town
ow and *ou:*	out, crown

🔤 Explore Phonics

Use these activities to help children explore vowel digraphs and diphthongs.

• **Word Ladders with Digraphs *ea* and *oo*** Write words that have the vowel digraph *ea*, including *tea* and *bread*, on index cards. Tape the cards along the bottom of a wall. Then pass out the remaining cards to children. Help each child read the word and tape the card above the word with the matching vowel sound to form a "ladder." Repeat with the digraph *oo* using the words *book* and *moon*.

• **Word Walls with Digraphs *ue, ui, ew* and *au, aw, al*** Establish a word wall in which children contribute words they hear or read that have the digraphs *ue, ui,* and *ew.* Have children write words with *ue* on blue rectangles, words with *ui* on red rectangles, and words with *ew* on yellow rectangles. Repeat with the digraphs *au, aw,* and *al.*

• **Word Ladders with Vowel Diphthongs** Write words that have different vowel diphthongs on index cards. Include the key words found on each activity page. As each skill is introduced, tape the cards with the key words along the bottom of a wall. Then pass out the remaining cards to children. Help each child read the word and tape the card above the word with the matching vowel sound and spelling pattern to form a "ladder."

📖 Develop Vocabulary and Meaning

Words with Vowel Digraphs and Diphthongs

ea:	eat, head
oo:	book, food, good, looked, soon, spoon, too
ue, ui, and *ew:*	juice, new, stew, Sue, true
au, aw, and *al:*	all, laugh, yawn
oy:	enjoy (There are no words with *oi* in the story.)
ow:	bowl, know, tomorrow
ow and *ou:*	found (There are no words with *ow* in the story.)

High-Frequency Words

a, all, and, at, by, come, could, do, don't, give, had, have, her, I, in, is, it, like, me, of, or, said, she, some, the, this, to, too, was, will, with, you

Story Words

There are many story words. Review the story to choose the words which children in your class will find most difficult.

Vocabulary Words

close, enjoy, laugh, quick, right, sick, stare, well

The following activities will help prepare children for reading the unit story independently. Afterwards, children can complete the vocabulary exercise on page 144.

• **A Bowl of Stew** Write the words from the vocabulary lists on the previous page on vegetable-shaped cutouts. Introduce the words and use each in a sentence. Then glue the cutouts to a large circle cut out of mural paper. Tell children the words are part of a bowl of stew. Invite children to take turns tossing a beanbag on the vegetables, spelling the words, and reading them aloud. Children can track the words using a list written on the chalkboard or on a list they write.

• **Synonyms** Explain that some words can have the same or almost the same meanings. Challenge children to name synonyms for the following words: *shut (close), happy (glad), yell (shout), look (see).*

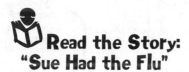

Read the Story: "Sue Had the Flu"

Before Reading

Display the cover of the book and read the title. Invite children to tell about times they were sick and what they did to get better. Then ask children to follow along in their books as you read the story to see what Sue does to get well.

During Reading

• **Model Fluency** As you read the story aloud, model the fluency skills of reading rhymes and reading quotations.

• **Model Comprehension** You may wish to model how to predict story events by making statements and asking questions based on illustrations.

After Reading

Have children find and read the words or phrases in the story that answer these questions:

How do you know that Sue did not feel well? (Answers will vary.)

What did Grandma bring to Sue? (juice and stew)

Do you think Sue will feel better when she wakes up? Why do you think as you do? (Answers will vary.)

Reread the Story: "Sue Had the Flu"

• **Oral Reading** Talk about dialogue and help children recognize that this story is a combination of narration and dialogue. The narration describes where Sue is and what she does. The dialogue tells what Sue and her grandmother say to each other. Point out the quotation marks and explain that these marks signal that someone is talking. Invite children to take turns reading aloud lines from the story. After a child has read a line, ask if the line was narration or dialogue. Have children identify the speaker if the sentence is dialogue.

• **Fluent Reading** Have children turn to page 4. Point out the quotation marks and explain that these marks signal that someone is talking. Read the sentences in the voice of a grandmother. Then turn to page 5. Read these sentences as a sick child. Discuss with children the importance of reading as the character. Then encourage children to rehearse the quotations.

Connect the Story to Writing

• **Write a Get-Well Card** Invite children to create get-well cards for Sue or for someone they know that is sick. Have them decorate their cards and write a message.

Support ESOL Learners

Help children understand the English expressions used when talking about illness—for example, "giving" an illness to someone, "catching" an illness, or "getting over" an illness.

At Home

Encourage children to read "Sue Had the Flu" with someone at home. Suggest that after reading they talk about the flu, favorite flu remedies, and ways to avoid getting it in the first place.

Name _____ Date _____

Vowel Digraph **ea**

t<u>ea</u>   br<u>ea</u>d

A **vowel digraph** is two vowels that are next to each other. The vowel digraph **ea** can stand for the **long e** sound in **tea** or the **short e** sound in **bread**.

Say each picture name. Write a word from the box that names the picture. Then circle the pictures whose names have the **short e** sound.

feather	jeans	peach	seal	sweater	thread

1	2	3

4	5	6

Write a sentence about the picture.

_____

_____

_____

_____

Vowel Digraph oo

book   **raccoon**

A **vowel digraph** is two vowels that are next to each other. The vowel digraph **oo** can stand for the sound you hear in **book** or the sound you hear in **raccoon**.

Say each picture name. Write a word from the box that names the picture. Then circle the pictures whose names have the same sound as **book**.

hook	moon	stool	tooth	wood	wool

1
_____

2
_____

3
_____

4
_____

5
_____

6
_____

Write a sentence about the picture.

_____

_____

_____

_____

Rhyming Riddles with Vowel Digraphs **ea** and **oo**

Read each clue. Think about the word in dark print. Write a word that rhymes with that word to solve the riddle. The first one is done for you.

1 What do you call something that a **cook** reads?

A c o o k   b o o k

2 What do you call the food that a **seal** eats?

A s e a l   __ __ __ __

3 What does a **raccoon** eat with?

A r a c c o o n

__ __ __ __ __ __

4 What do you call the jelly or jam that you put on **bread**?

A b r e a d

__ __ __ __ __ __ __

5 What kind of **wood** burns well?

A __ __ __ __ __ __   w o o d

6 What kind of **goose** can run away?

A __ __ __ __ __ __

g o o s e

Vowel Digraphs **ue**, **ui**, and **ew**

blue   fruit   chew

The vowel digraphs **ue**, **ui**, and **ew** can all stand for the same sound.

Say each picture name. Write a word from the box that names the picture.

clue	glue	juice	screw	stew	suit

1

2

3

4

5

6

Write a sentence about the picture.

fruit

_____
_____
_____
_____

Vowel Digraphs au, aw, and al

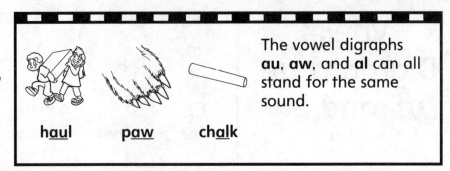

haul   paw   chalk

The vowel digraphs **au**, **aw**, and **al** can all stand for the same sound.

Say each picture name. Write a word from the box that names the picture.

| crawl | faucet | hall | saucer | talk | yawn |

Write a sentence about the picture.

_____
- - - - - - - - - - - - -
_____
- - - - - - - - - - - - -
_____

Name _____   Date _____

Riddles with Vowel Digraphs

Write a word from the box to answer each riddle.

clues   glue   juice   mall   stew   straw   wall

1

What is a kind of fruit drink? _____

2

What is sticky and can hold things together? _____

3

Where can you go shopping? _____

4

What can you use to sip a drink? _____

5

What kind of food do you
make with meat and vegetables? _____

6

What does a detective look for? _____

7

What can you make with bricks? _____

Review Vowel Digraphs

Darken the circle beside the word that completes each sentence.
Then write the word on the line.

1 Jean and Paul went to see the animals at the
_____
_ _ _ _ _ _ _ _ _ _ _ _
_____ .
- ○ zoo
- ○ school
- ○ stool

2
_____
_ _ _ _ _ _ _ _ _ _ _ _
They saw a _____ swim through
the water.
- ○ peach
- ○ bread
- ○ seal

3
_____
_ _ _ _ _ _ _ _ _ _ _ _
They saw a bear with sharp _____ .
- ○ salts
- ○ saucers
- ○ claws

4
_____
_ _ _ _ _ _ _ _ _ _ _
It was eating _____ for its meal.
- ○ meat
- ○ thread
- ○ spread

5
_____
_ _ _ _ _ _ _ _ _ _
The bear did not _____ its food.
- ○ chew
- ○ blue
- ○ juice

6
_____
_ _ _ _ _ _ _ _ _ _
Jean saw a _____ group of penguins.
- ○ stalk
- ○ crawl
- ○ small

7 The penguins looked like they wore black and
_ _ _ _ _ _ _ _ _ _ _
white _____ .
- ○ stews
- ○ glues
- ○ suits

8 Jean and Paul also saw monkeys swing on
_____
_ _ _ _ _ _ _ _ _ _ _
_____ .
- ○ moons
- ○ cooks
- ○ hoops

Diphthongs oi and oy

coins   boy

A **diphthong** is two vowels blended together to make one vowel sound. The diphthongs **oi** and **oy** stand for the same vowel sound.

Say each picture name. Write a word from the box that names the picture.

| boil   foil   joy   oil   point   toys |

1

_____

2

_____

3

_____

4

_____

5

_____

6

_____

Write a sentence about the picture.

_____

_____

_____

The Sounds of **ow**

The letters **ow** can stand for the **long o** sound in **bowl** or the **diphthong** in **owl**.

b<u>ow</u>l   <u>ow</u>l

Say each picture name. Write a word from the box that names the picture. Then circle the pictures whose names have the **long o** sound.

| blow   cow   frown   mow   snow   town |

1

_____
_ _ _ _ _ _ _ _ _
_____

2

_____
_ _ _ _ _ _ _ _ _
_____

3

_____
_ _ _ _ _ _ _ _ _
_____

4

_____
_ _ _ _ _ _ _ _ _
_____

5

_____
_ _ _ _ _ _ _ _ _
_____

6

_____
_ _ _ _ _ _ _ _ _
_____

Write a sentence about the picture.

_____
_ _ _ _ _ _ _ _ _ _ _ _ _ _ _ _
_____
_ _ _ _ _ _ _ _ _ _ _ _ _ _ _ _
_____

Diphthongs ow and ou

cow   mouse

A **diphthong** is two vowels blended together to make one vowel sound. The diphthongs **ow** and **ou** can stand for the same vowel sound.

Say each picture name. Write a word from the box that names the picture.

clown	crown	couch	frown	mouth	scout

1
_____

2
_____

3
_____

4
_____

5
_____

6
_____

Write a sentence about the picture.

_____
_____
_____

Word Find with Diphthongs

Read the words in the box. Find each word in the puzzle and circle it. The words go across and down.

boys	crow	down	enjoy	flower
grow	house	howl	mouse	mow
noise	point	shout	soil	toy

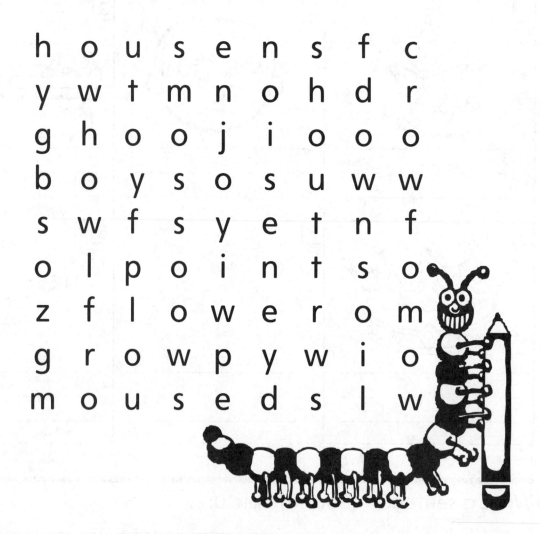

```
h  o  u  s  e  n  s  f  c
y  w  t  m  n  o  h  d  r
g  h  o  o  j  i  o  o  o
b  o  y  s  o  s  u  w  w
s  w  f  s  y  e  t  n  f
o  l  p  o  i  n  t  s  o
z  f  l  o  w  e  r  o  m
g  r  o  w  p  y  w  i  o
m  o  u  s  e  d  s  l  w
```

Name _____ Date _____

Review Diphthongs

Darken the circle beside the word that completes each sentence. Then write the word on the line.

1

_____

Circus fans make a lot of _____ .

○ noise
○ coins
○ toys

2

_____

The _____ cheers loudly.

○ cloud
○ crown
○ crowd

3

_____

The children are full of _____ .

○ coils
○ boy
○ joy

4

_____

Some people jump up and _____ .

○ down
○ mow
○ cow

5

_____

They laugh at the funny _____ .

○ found
○ clowns
○ round

6

_____

Everyone _____ to the people who fly through the air.

○ joints
○ joins
○ points

7

_____

The fans _____ each part of the circus.

○ enjoy
○ oil
○ soil

8

_____

No one can _____ at a circus.

○ frown
○ brown
○ hound

Phonics, Second Grade SV 8862-5

Vocabulary

Read each sentence. Write a word from the box that has the same or almost the same meaning as the underlined word.

close	enjoy	laugh	quick
right	sick	stare	well

1 Drew was feeling <u>ill</u>.

_____

2 He did not <u>giggle</u> or play.

_____

3 All he could do was sit and <u>look</u> at the wall.

_____

4 Drew did not <u>like</u> feeling this way.

_____

5 "Do not get <u>next</u> to me!" Drew told his brother.

_____

6 Drew was <u>fast</u> to cover his nose and mouth when he sneezed.

_____

7 Drew ate stew and felt <u>good</u>.

_____

8 "Eating stew was the <u>correct</u> thing to do," Drew said.

_____

Sue Had the Flu

Sue ate the stew.
She found that Grandma was right.
After giving a yawn,
Sue slept through the night.

Sue had the flu.
She was sick in bed.
Sue didn't feel good
from her toes to her head.

"Thanks," said Sue.
"I will eat this stew.
I know by tomorrow
I will feel like new."

Soon Grandma came back
with a bowl and a spoon.
"Eat all of this food,
and you will feel better soon!"

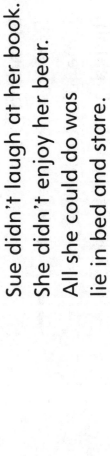

Sue didn't laugh at her book.
She didn't enjoy her bear.
All she could do was
lie in bed and stare.

Grandma looked at Sue.
"Is it true you are sick?
Some juice and some stew
should get you well quick."

"I have a fever and a cough.
I think I have the flu.
Don't get too close to me,
or I might give it to you."

Word Wheel

Cut out each wheel. Attach with a brad.

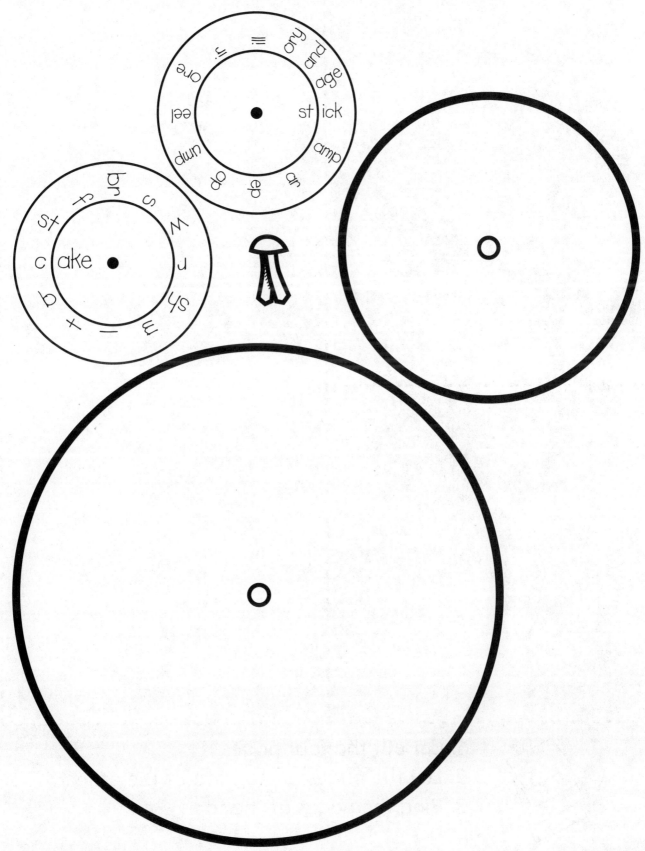

Step Book

1. Cut out the four pages.
2. Lay the pages one on top of the other.
3. Bind the pages at the top.

Flip Book

Cut out the book back and the pages. Staple the pages to the book back.

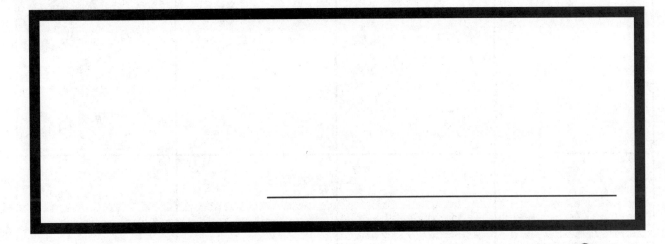

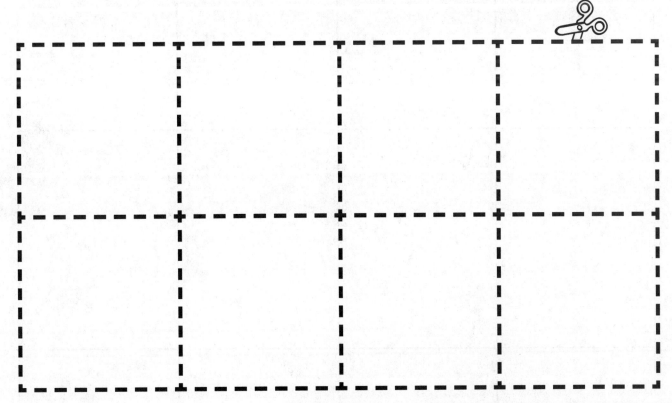

Name _____ Date _____

Grid

Blackline Master 4
Phonics, Second Grade SV 8862-5

Name _____ Date _____

Graph

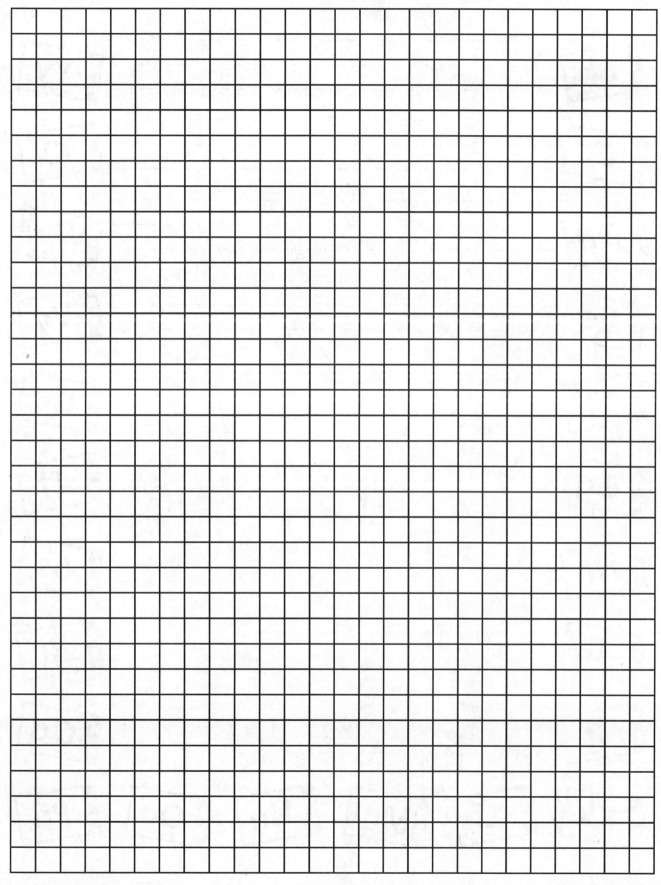

Blackline Master 5

Phonics, Second Grade SV 8862-5

Name _____   Date _____

Writer's Dictionary

www.svschoolsupply.com

© Harcourt Achieve Inc.

Blackline Master 6
Phonics, Second Grade SV 8862-5

Phonics Plus, Second Grade
Answer Key

Page 5
1. pet
2. dog
3. like
4. home
5. car
6. house
7. joy
8. new

Page 6
1. store
2. grapes
3. plums
4. white
5. knife
6. wrap
7. snack
8. grand

Page 10
1. j or p
2. m
3. k
4. f
5. r
6. s
7. g
8. y
9. w
10. p
11. l
12. b
13. n
14. v
15. d
16. h

Page 11
Children color the parts with these words: *squirrel, rabbit, kitten, hen, lamb, goat, pony, calf,* and *horse.* The hidden picture is a fish.

ABC order: calf, goat, hen, horse, kitten, lamb, pony, rabbit, and squirrel.

Page 12
1. k
2. d
3. t
4. m
5. x
6. r
7. s
8. n
9. p or g
10. l
11. f
12. m
13. v
14. g
15. l
16. b

Page 13
1. Children write *t* in *cat, sat,* and *hat.*
2. Children write *k* in *Look, cook,* and *milk.*
3. Children write *s* in *bus, stops,* and *gas.*
4. Children write *g* in *big, frog,* and *log.*
5. Children write *d* in *said, food,* and *good.*
6. Children write *n* in hen, *fun, in,* and *sun.*

Page 14
1. m
2. g
3. v
4. z
5. x
6. b
7. p
8. l
9. n
10. c
11. t
12. d

Page 15
1. shovel
2. river
3. lemon
4. camel
5. robot
6. table

Page 16
1. zoo
2. pal
3. bus
4. sun
5. tiger
6. seal
7. water
8. wet

Page 17
Children circle the following pictures:
1. pencil, fence
2. cap, can
3. lace, ice
4. celery, face

Page 18
1. cat
2. ice
3. cub
4. cent
5. coat

Page 19
Children circle the following pictures:
1. giant, gem
2. gum, girl
3. hedge, badge
4. pig, guitar

Page 20
1. giant
2. pig
3. gerbil
4. page
5. fudge
6. goldfish
7. hedge
8. stage

Question: giraffes

Page 21
Children circle the following pictures:
1. bus, mask
2. fuse, peas
3. tissue, sugar
4. vase, dress

Page 22
Children color the parts with these words: *see, bus, sit, dress, sad, sing, kiss, said, gas,* and *yes.* The hidden picture is a sock. Sentences will vary, but should include the word *sock.*

Page 23
1. city
2. mice
3. garden
4. hedge
5. stops
6. sure
7. rose
8. peas

Page 24
1. b
2. a
3. a
4. b
5. a
6. b

Page 32

Children write **a** under
these pictures:

1. ax   6. cap
3. pan   7. mask
4. gas   8. bag

Sentences will vary, but
children could include the
words *cat* and *apple*.

Page 33

Children color the boxes in
this order: *hat, ant, can, fan,
ax, bat, cap, van,* and *hand.*
The cat spilled the milk.

Page 34

Children write **o** under these
pictures:

1. box   5. doll
2. pot   7. mop
4. lock   8. ostrich

Sentences will vary, but
children could include the
words *frog* and *olives.*

Page 35

1. sock   4. cot
2. doll   5. pop
3. clock 6. top

Page 36

Children write **i** under these
pictures:

1. pin   5. fish
3. bib   6. pig
4. lip   7. igloo

Sentences will vary, but
children could include the
words *chick* and *ink.*

Page 37

Children color the following
rhyming word pairs:

1. hit, pit   6. did, hid
2. pin, fin 7. win, pin
3. lid, hid   8. bill, will
4. pill, hill 9. him, dim
5. pig, dig 10. sit, bit

Page 38

1. cat   5. ran
2. top   6. hid
3. milk   7. job
4. drip   8. mop

Page 39

Children write **u** under
these pictures:

1. bug   4. rug
2. gum   5. cut
3. bus   8. umpire

Sentences will vary, but
children could include the
words *duck* and *up.*

Page 40

Across	Down
1. tub	1. truck
3. gum	2. bug
5. up	4. mug
6. duck	6. drum
7. skunk	

Page 41

Children write **e** under these
pictures:

1. bed   5. exit
2. web   6. hen
4. net   8. bell

Sentences will vary, but
children could include the
words *nest* and *eggs.*

Page 42

Children color the parts
with these words: *bed, dress,
web, nest, ten, bell, desk, jet,
sled,* and *pen.* The hidden
picture is a bell. Sentences
will vary, but children
should include the word
bell.

Page 43

1. Ten   5. legs
2. jumped 6. went
3. mud   7. mess
4. rest   8. tub

Page 44

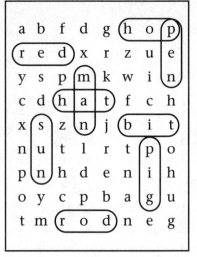

Rhyming words will vary.

Page 45

1. pig   5. hot
2. dig   6. bath
3. mud   7. wet
4. tub   8. rag

Page 46

1. looks 4. twigs
2. twists 5. string
3. picks

Page 54

Children write **a** and **e**
under these pictures:

1. cane   6. cape
2. ape   7. race
4. vase   8. wave

Sentences will vary, but
children could include the
words *ape* and *cape.*

Page 55

Children circle and write
the following words:

1. sail   4. tray
2. nail   5. rain
3. pay   6. jay

Sentences will vary, but
children could include the
words *quail* and *hay.*

Page 56

1. space 4. pail
2. grape 5. ray
3. pay

Page 57

Children write **o** and **e** under these pictures:

1. rope
3. robe
4. mole
5. hose
6. bone
8. nose

Sentences will vary, but children could include the words *mole* and *rose*.

Page 58

Children circle and write the following words:

1. road
2. toe
3. boat
4. toad
5. mow
6. doe

Sentences will vary, but children could include the words *doe* and *road*.

Page 59

1. hoe
2. toe
3. joke
4. poke
5. hole
6. pole
7. rose
8. nose
9. row
10. low

Page 60

Children write **i** and **e** under these pictures:

1. bike
2. five
5. dive
6. ice
7. nine
8. kite

Sentences will vary, but children could include the words *mice* and *ice*.

Page 61

Children circle and write the following words:

1. tie
2. vine
3. lie
4. pies
5. die
6. slide

Sentences will vary, but children could include the words *five* and *pies*.

Page 62

Children color these kites:

1. vine, fine, pine
2. hike, bike, like
3. pie, lie, die
5. mice, nice, ice
6. ripe, pipe, wipe
7. fries, ties, pies
10. dive, five, hive

Page 63

1. side
2. hoe
3. rake
4. roses
5. row
6. ripe
7. bowl
8. pie

Page 64

Children write **u** and **e** under these pictures:

1. flute
3. dune
4. tube
5. glue
6. June
8. fuse

Sentences will vary, but children could include the words *mule* and *flute*.

Page 65

1. cube
2. tune
3. glue
4. tube
5. fuse
6. mule
7. prune
8. flute

Page 66

Children circle and write the following words:

1. eat (ea)
2. peas (ea)
3. feet (ee)
4. tree (ee)
5. sleep (ee)
6. seal (ea)

Sentences will vary, but children could include the words *bee* and *leaf*.

Page 67

1. seat
2. bean
3. weed
4. bee
5. read
6. heel
7. leaf

Riddle: a needle

Page 68

Children color the boxes in this order: *toe, cube, hay, road, pie, team, nail, see,* and *time.* The mice live in the tree stump.

Page 69

1. grow
2. home
3. seeds
4. need
5. use
6. day
7. side
8. fine

Page 70

1. to
2. sea
3. its
4. two
5. see
6. it's

Page 78

1. (stamp) st
2. (spider) sp
3. (skates) sk
4. (slide) sl
5. (square) sq
6. (snail) sn
7. (sweater) sw
8. (smoke) sm

Sentences will vary, but children could include the words *slide, sweater,* and *scarf.*

Page 79

1. snail
2. smile
3. store
4. swan
5. skirt

Riddle: a star

Page 80

1. (pretzel) pr
2. (frog) fr
3. (crib) cr
4. (truck) tr
5. (bread) br
6. (dress) dr
7. (grapes) gr
8. (brick) br

Sentences will vary, but children could include the words *dress* and *grapes.*

Page 81

1. brush
2. train
3. broom
4. drip
5. crown
6. crane

Page 82

1. (clock) cl
2. (glass) gl
3. (block) bl
4. (sled) sl
5. (flute) fl
6. (plate) pl
7. (globe) gl
8. (clown) cl

Sentences will vary, but children could include the words *clown* and *blocks*.

Page 83

1. clock
2. flat
3. slow
4. sled
5. play
6. clown

Page 84

Children write **tw** under the following pictures:

1. twelve
4. twine
5. twins
7. tweezers
8. twist

Sentences will vary, but children could include the words *twins* and *twelve*.

Page 85

1. blow
2. trees
3. clouds
4. sky
5. storm
6. drops
7. ground
8. place

Page 86

1. (mask) sk
2. (quilt) lt
3. (lamp) mp
4. (ant) nt
5. (hand) nd
6. (tent) nt
7. (vest) st
8. (belt) lt

Sentences will vary, but children could include the words *tent* and *lamp*.

Page 87

Children circle the last two letters in the following words:

1a. went
1b. west
1c. vest
1d. vent
1e. dent
2a. disk
2b. dusk
2c. tusk
2d. task
2e. tank
3a. land
3b. lend
3c. bend
3d. bent
3e. cent

Page 88

Children circle the last two letters in the following words:

1. bank
2. stamp
3. breakfast
4. band
5. vest
6. stump
7. belt
8. desk

Page 89

1. camp
2. pond
3. best
4. tent
5. lamp
6. quilt
7. dusk
8. felt

Page 90

1. fluffy
2. tower
3. crown
4. snuck
5. flash
6. shapes
7. scare
8. frown

Page 98

1. (whistle) wh
2. (cherry) ch
3. (whiskers) wh
4. (chick) ch
5. (wheel) wh
6. (children) ch
7. (whisper) wh
8. (chain) ch

Sentences will vary, but children could include the words *children* and *whisper*.

Page 99

1. chain
2. chick
3. wheel
4. wheat
5. chin
6. cherry

Riddle: a chair

Page 100

1. (shirt) sh
2. (thermometer) th
3. (ship) sh
4. (thermos) th
5. (sheep) sh
6. (shark) sh
7. (thorn) th
8. (thirteen) th

Sentences will vary, but children could include the words *shirt* and *thirteen*.

Page 101

Across	Down
2. thumb	1. think
4. shark	3. shovel
6. shell	5. thorn
7. shirt	

Page 102

1. (knob) kn
2. (wrist) wr
3. (wreath) wr
4. (knife) kn
5. (wrench) wr
6. (wrap) wr
7. (knee) kn
8. (knot) kn

Sentences will vary, but children could include the words *knight* and *write*.

Page 103

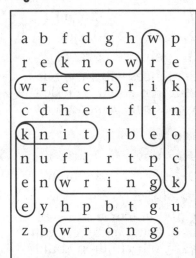

Page 104

1. ship
2. whale
3. shark
4. chase
5. when
6. thirty
7. wreath
8. knock

Page 105

1. (bench) ch
2. (bath) th
3. (wrench) ch
4. (moth) th
5. (peach) ch
6. (wreath) th
7. (teach) ch
8. (math) th

Sentences will vary, but children could include the words *teeth* and *peach*.

Page 106

1. (skunk) nk
2. (swing) ng
3. (trunk) nk
4. (fang) ng
5. (bank) nk
6. (bunk) nk
7. (sing) ng
8. (wing) ng

Sentences will vary, but children could include the words *skunk* and *sing*.

Page 107

1. (brush) sh
2. (match) tch
3. (chick) ck
4. (leash) sh
5. (clock) ck
6. (wash) sh
7. (catch) tch
8. (duck) ck

Sentences will vary, but children could include the words *wash* and *sock*.

Page 108

Children circle the last two letters in the following words:

1a. sock
1b. song
1c. wrong
1d. wring
1e. ring
2a. wish
2b. wash
2c. watch
2d. patch
2e. pitch
3a. catch
3b. watch
3c. wash
3d. wish
3e. wink

Page 109

1. children
2. fish
3. shoes
4. splash
5. knee
6. Ouch
7. shovel
8. whistles

Page 110

1. day; Children draw a line to the sun in the sky.
2. outside; Children draw a line to the yard.
3. beautiful; Children draw a line to the house.
4. play; Children draw a line to the children playing a game.
5. catch; Children draw a line to the glove catching the ball.
6. sleeping; Children draw a line to the child sleeping.

Page 118

Children write the following letter pairs:

1. (fork) or
2. (star) ar
3. (horse) or
4. (jar) ar
5. (yarn) ar
6. (horn) or
7. (thorn) or
8. (shark) ar

Sentences will vary, but children could include the words *barn* and *horse*.

Page 119

Children circle and write the following words:

1. purse
2. stir
3. herd
4. girl
5. church
6. surf

Sentences will vary, but children could include the words *nurse*, *bird*, and *fern*.

Page 120

1. barn, church, park, fort, yard
2. stork, shark, horse, bird, lark
3. horn, snarl, organ, harp, chirp, purr, snort
4. barn, horse, corn, dirt, herd
5. spur, shorts, scarf, shirt, skirt

Page 121

1. farm
2. corn
3. horses
4. barn
5. dirt
6. birds
7. cart
8. porch

Page 122

Children circle and write the following words:

1. sky
2. baby
3. lady
4. cry
5. dry
6. penny

Children circle the baby crawling, the lady, and the penny.
Sentences will vary, but children could include the words *puppy* and *fly*.

Page 123

1. happy
2. twenty
3. bunny
4. puppy
5. tiny
6. Baby
7. cry
8. shy

Page 124

1. farmer; Children draw a line to the farmer.
2. socks; Children draw a line to the socks.
3. chores; Children draw a line to the boy mowing.
4. hurry; Children draw a line to the girl that is running.
5. clouds; Children draw a line to the picture of the clouds.
6. sky; Children draw a line to the picture of the moon and stars in the night sky.

Page 132

1. jeans
2. feather
3. peach
4. seal
5. thread
6. sweater

Children circle the feather, thread, and sweater.
Sentences will vary, but children could include the words *eat*, *tea*, and *bread*.

Page 133

1. moon
2. hook
3. stool
4. wool
5. tooth
6. wood

Children circle the hook, wool, and wood.
Sentences will vary, but children could include the words *book*, *moon*, and *raccoon*.

Page 134

1. cook
2. meal
3. spoon
4. spread
5. good
6. loose

Page 135

1. suit
2. screw
3. glue
4. stew
5. clue
6. juice

Sentences will vary, but children could include the words *blueberries*, *fruit*, and *chew*.

Page 136

1. talk
2. faucet
3. yawn
4. crawl
5. saucer
6. hall

Sentences will vary, but children could include the words *yawn*, *walk*, and *hall*.

Page 137

1. juice
2. glue
3. mall
4. straw
5. stew
6. clues
7. wall

Page 138

1. zoo
2. seal
3. claws
4. meat
5. chew
6. small
7. suits
8. hoops

Page 139

1. boil
2. toys
3. point
4. foil
5. joy
6. oil

Sentences will vary, but children could include the words *boy*, *point*, and *coins*.

Page 140

1. snow
2. cow
3. frown
4. town
5. blow
6. mow

Children circle snow, blow, and mow. Sentences will vary, but children could include the words *snow* and *town*.

Page 141

1. clown
2. frown
3. couch
4. crown
5. scout
6. mouth

Sentences will vary, but children could include the words *cow*, *mouse*, and *couch*.

Page 142

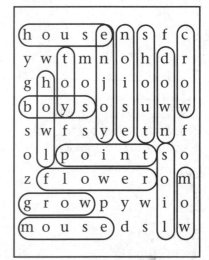

Page 143

1. noise
2. crowd
3. joy
4. down
5. clowns
6. points
7. enjoy
8. frown

Page 144

1. sick
2. laugh
3. stare
4. enjoy
5. close
6. quick
7. well
8. right